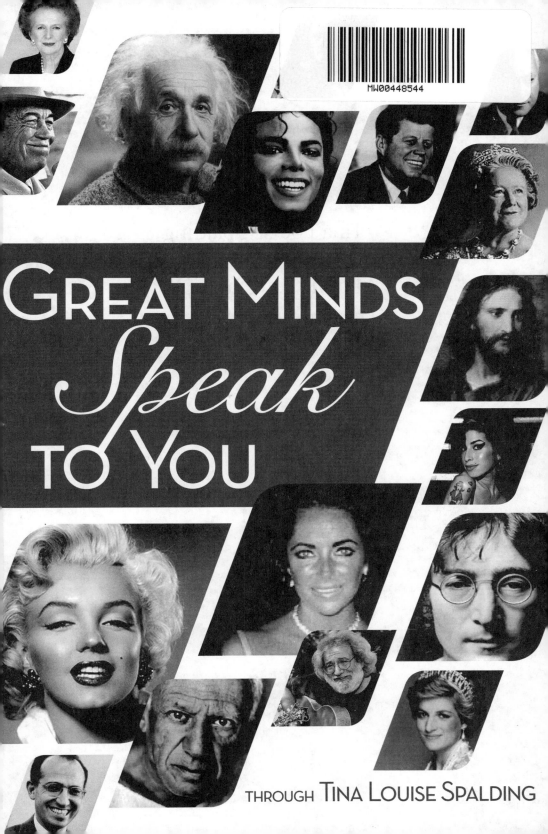

GREAT MINDS
Speak
TO YOU

THROUGH TINA LOUISE SPALDING

Other Books by
Tina Louise Spalding

Making Love to GOD:
The Path to Divine Sex

GREAT MINDS
Speak
TO YOU

THROUGH TINA LOUISE SPALDING

LIGHT Technology PUBLISHING

ISBN: 978-1-62233-010-2

PUBLISHING

PO Box 3540
Flagstaff, AZ 86003
1-800-450-0985
1-928-526-1345
www.lighttechnology.com

This book is dedicated to all the channels who have inspired me over the years and have been brave enough to speak their truth for all of us to hear. Especially dear to my heart are Jane Roberts, Neale Donald Walsh, Esther Hicks, and Helen Schucman, whose books, recordings, and tapes have helped to inspire and encourage me on my own journey.

CONTENTS

PREFACE

IT HAS BEEN ALMOST A YEAR NOW since Ananda came into my life, waking me up and shaking my world to the core. Ananda is a group of nonphysical beings who have been speaking through me on a daily basis through channeling. They are now teaching regularly here on the island on which I live, and slowly but surely, word of their presence is spreading. They have been speaking on many subjects — from sexuality to religion, education, and food — and it is becoming clear that we face many challenges in our transformation from sleep to waking, from fear to love. But they assure me and all who come to chat with them that this is why they are here: to help us on our waking journey, to assist us as we walk toward the light.

Two days ago I was told that I would be starting another book — this book, the second that I have penned for Ananda as their channel. The concept — speaking to famous departed beings — was quite a surprise, I have to say. It is not something I was expecting, and to be quite honest, the form and subject matter made me just a little nervous. But let me start the story where it began: just two short weeks ago.

My youngest sister received a phone call when we were together one afternoon. She was told by a sad and weeping voice that a good friend had died suddenly and had just been found in his apartment. Tears were shed, and with stunned faces we made a valiant attempt to carry on, but there had been a loss, and my sister was hit hard by the news.

The following weekend she went to Vancouver for her friend's memorial and was deeply saddened, sobbing throughout the service. When she came back, she came to visit me one evening to tell me all about her trip and what had transpired. About an hour before she arrived at my house, I tuned into Ananda — as I usually do before they do a reading for someone — and they made an unusual statement: "There is someone here who wishes to speak to your sister." I was stunned, to say the least. Ananda continued, "It is her dear friend Malcolm, who has recently passed. He wants to talk to your sister and tell her about his death experience."

I was quite shocked, as you can imagine, having never spoken for anyone other than Ananda up until that point. I told Ananda that I would like to "chat" with Malcolm first, before my sister arrived, and we all agreed that yes, he would speak to me and through me so that I could decide for myself if I wanted to do this. I should explain here that by "to me and through me," I mean that this nonphysical energy would use my voice to communicate, and I would record the event so that I could listen to what was said.

You see, when I am channeling in this way, my recollection is poor, and to really get what has transpired I must listen to a recording of the spoken exchange. Ananda has told me that because the thoughts and ideas are not generated by my mind but only passing through my brain, the recollection is weak. Often it's like trying to remember a dream; sometimes only snippets remain.

So Malcolm spoke to me, through me, asking for permission to speak to my younger sister, his friend. I was nervous about this turn of events. I was talking to dead people, and the cogs in my mind began to churn, giving me a feeling of what can only be described as slight panic.

When my sister arrived, I was looking a little shaken, and as she came in the house she asked if I was okay.

"Have I got a surprise for you!" I said as she came into the living room. "Malcolm wants to talk to you."

She was very excited and quite unflustered by it all. You see, she has had dozens of chats with Ananda, and they have become her dear friends and spiritual mentors. I played her the recording with Malcolm I had so recently made, and she was fascinated.

So I tuned in to Ananda again, and they spoke to my sister, telling her that Malcolm wanted to talk about his transition through what we call death. So that is what he did. My sister and Malcolm chatted for about fifty minutes or so. Malcolm was very animated and joyful about his death experience and the limited events he'd been exposed to so far in the new environment he now found himself in. He spoke with a strong British accent, as he had in life. My sister was happy and moved to talk to her friend. I, on the other hand, was quite shaken by it all, but Ananda assured me that all would be well. They said I should trust and relax.

All in all, it was a dramatic evening for both of us — each for different reasons, of course. Ananda assured me that this was a great gift I was being offered and that there would be many such exchanges in my future, that this would become part of my work here, re-educating people on the close and dynamic connection to Spirit that we can have if we come to understand death, dying, and communications with the nonphysical.

Whoa! Really? What was going on here? I was confused and a little nervous about this new turn of events, but they weren't finished yet. Apparently this experience with Malcolm was only an introduction to a whole new world of nonphysical communication that I was about to enter.

The following day, I was informed of yet another nonphysical intelligence wishing to speak to me: a famous person had passed over, someone with a message for us, someone we would recognize. Ananda told me that this new book would be called *Great Minds Speak to You* and that there was a long line of departed beings who had something to say. I don't think I was really able to comprehend what I was in for in those initial discussions, but this is a transcription of Ananda's description of this new project as they spoke to me that day:

We are with you again, dear one. Indeed, it seems fantastic, does it not, that a being who you would consider to be extremely famous wishes to speak through you? However, there is once again our argument that once you have established contact with the nonphysical, once you have established contact with beings who are not restricted by your three-dimensional time and space, you have access to many minds indeed.

These beings do not walk around for decades as particular personalities that you would recognize as particular characters; however, the concepts, mind, passions, and dreams of that particular being you recognize as Albert Einstein still remain "in a packet," you would say, in a conglomeration that can be tapped into. His passion did not die with his body, for he was not his body. He was a physical focus point of a particular desire, of particular talents, and these remain. They remain for anybody to tap in to. His oversoul exists still and has access to this particular realm of existence that was manifested as Albert Einstein, this magnificent scientist, mathematician, and philosopher.

And so you are able to tap into this knowledge through subtle direction from us. We are not instigating it, per se; there is a desire within the oversoul of that particular being to communicate with the world, so this is what is happening.

So we wish you to just stay open minded. There are going to be many communications from many different beings, and you will feel a difference. You will be able to see that they are not the same person. They are not us, Ananda. You will discern them as different entities, and we hope that you will enjoy this experience, for there are many who wish to speak to you, who wish to speak through you, and who wish to pass along information related to their subject, related to their experience in their bodies, in their passing, and in their current world of experience as nonphysical beings.

We will just ask you to relax and prepare yourself to channel this information. This is going to be a book. We wish for you to keep track of this information. As we said, each one of these beings who come through you has something to say to the world, and they are speaking from their hearts to the hearts of all on the planet. This is important work, dear one, and we hope that you are able to relax, to enjoy it, and to welcome it as a wonderful experience.

Do not judge what this will look like. Now you feel as if this will invite ridicule, but you must understand that it will not. The wisdom contained within these words is going to be inspiring, it is going to be enthralling, and you will find that this book will be received very well indeed.

So sit back and relax. We will carry on with our work from this side, and you will indeed experience the concepts of Albert Einstein as he speaks to you, through your body, in this intriguing and unusual way.

INTRODUCTION

ANANDA

HERE WE ARE, dear ones, with a new project for you to enjoy and explore. This is going to be a treatise from several great minds who have lived on your Earth plane and have had some wonderful experiences they wish to share. We explain this book in this way.

Your culture has had a great love affair with the famous and infamous, and indeed, it continues and strengthens as you experience your mass media and digital forms of communication. It has been decided by this particular group of beings, in combination with our ideas and desire, to write this book as a selection of opinions and ideas from those who had some notoriety on your planet and who wished to tell of their experiences in passing through the death experience, as well as their thoughts on what they have experienced since that passing. They also wish to share their highest and clearest ideals as they refer to your experience on this plane in this time called the twenty-first century.

Many in spirit look on these times of difficulty, abundance, trouble, and innovation and wish to share with you their experiences and ideas, so that is the project. Some famous names and faces will come to mind as you read this book, and you will glean some fine information about their own learning, their own suffering, and indeed their own experience in the life after this life, for they all wish to tell you that there is no death as you perceive it to be. They are all there in their astral forms, enjoying their continued growth, their continued expansion, and their continued joy in living.

Their messages are as varied as their lives were, and our purpose is this: For you to understand your true nature, your true potential, you must let go of your fear of death, for it makes you afraid to live. It causes you to rush and panic, to become scared, and to become paralyzed. If you truly understood that you are eternal beings, forgiven for all your errors and blamed for nothing that you would call a sin, you would open your hearts and minds to so much more and enjoy yourselves so much more. You would not suffer so at the loss of your loved ones, and you would work less and achieve more, for when you are in fear and grief, you are not yourselves and cannot achieve the goals that you have set for yourselves before you decided to be born onto this plane you call life.

Do as we have asked our dear one: Read this with an open mind and heart, and hear what these beings have to say. You have revered and reviled them in life; now let them complete their stories in what you call death, for that is the complete story, is it not? Telling of their lives is only the half of it, and only when you truly grasp this truth — that you live on forever — only then will you be able to be truly happy, truly free.

We are Ananda, your dear and challenging friends, pushing you out of your comfort zone, with love and affection always.

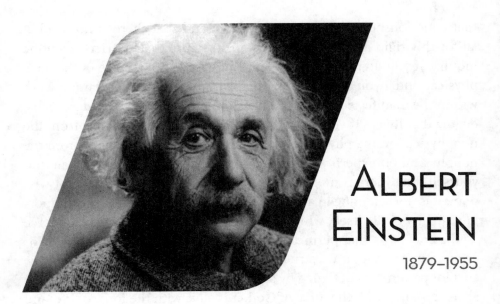

ALBERT
EINSTEIN
1879–1955

Albert Einstein was a German-born physicist who developed the theory of relativity. He is considered the most influential physicist of the twentieth century.

I HAVE BEEN HERE quite a while now. I passed over decades ago, but my work continues here. We work together as scientists and mathematicians on understanding the functioning processes of this universe. We all work together here and send information to Earth, to the scientists, mathematicians, teachers, and beings who are presently working on your plane to comprehend the processes of the universe and how they work.

We are very excited at some of the developments that are happening on your planet at this time. The understanding of the time-space continuum is very exciting, and we send many ideas down from this plane to the minds of those who are physically incarnated. We send mathematical theorems, physics philosophies, ideas, and the germs of ideas into the minds of those who are open to them. There are many scientists now who are spiritual in nature. This is the solution to many of your problems: to remove yourselves from the materialistic beliefs of the scientific method and open up your minds and hearts to these other realms.

This is one of the reasons I am speaking at this time, so you can see that consciousness carries on after death and that there is no need at all for this rigid and uncompromising structure that restricts scientific inquiry. If you do not believe in Spirit, if you do not believe in the non-physical, and if you do not believe in the unmanifested, you cannot work within the manifested world; it's that simple. You are restricted to such a degree that it is as if you are blind. There is so much influence from the nonphysical on the physical world, there is so much influence from the nonphysical on experiments and the existing matrix in which you find yourself, that there is no room for this kind of ignorance. It is not wisdom; it is not scientific in any way, for you are ignoring the most important quality of life itself, which is the animating force, the very life force — the energy — that permeates all living and vibrating structures. For even though you look at a structure and say that it is not living within the current parameters designed by science, this does not mean that it is not alive. It is alive with the force of God, it is alive with the force of life, and life is contained within all structures, both scientific and physiological.

Life is contained within ideas. This is one of the largest concepts that scientists lack, this idea that your very thoughts have life force in them. Of course, this is not agreed on in scientific realms, although conversations are beginning around this idea that thoughts create in the realms of the esoteric and New Age thinking. Scientists do not believe in it, but the fact that they do not believe in it does not mean that it is not true. The thoughts scientists have in their minds often come from us in the nonphysical, so they cannot isolate themselves from this realm.

This is one of the reasons I would like to speak to you today, this concept that spirituality does not have a place in science. This is the largest handicap that scientists work with, and they could achieve so much more if they would meditate and pray before designing experiments and during the observation of experiments, asking for assistance in interpreting information and redesigning experiments. They indeed get ideas all the time from us, but the force and breadth of the potential information that is coming to them is limited extremely by their belief structures.

But of course, this has come from the history of religion, and it was important for science to be separated from religion. But you cannot separate one aspect of a culture from the soup in which it is immersed. These scientific experiments, these ideas, were hatched in a culture that was rigid in its thinking, that was caught in the untruths of religion, so these experiments and the foundation of science itself are questionable. These isolated concepts cannot be considered true when the influence of spirit, the influence of the nonphysical, is so massive in these worlds. To work in isolation without taking them into consideration is a folly indeed.

You will ask if I am indeed Albert Einstein. I am indeed Albert Einstein; I have been Albert Einstein for quite some time, so I make a joke of this. It seems as if beings on your plane require proof for beings to be recognized as the personalities they say they are. I will not go into proof-giving theorems here; there is no need for that. If you do not believe in the nonphysical, this is not going to speak to you in any way at all. So this is for those of you who do already believe that there is something else other than this physical life you call the third-dimensional world, for there are many dimensions, many ways and languages in which life speaks to you. There are many languages and dimensions in which life exists.

Investigate the spiritual world. Investigate your interior world, for it is through your interior world that you access these realms. As a scientist here in what you would consider the afterlife — although there is no "after" about it, for it is the same life — I am engaged in the same kinds of works, the same kinds of experiences. I merely have what you would consider an astral body rather than a physical body. The experience you have is so very limited because of your lack of belief in the nonphysical world. It is as if you are living your life with your hands and feet tied, thinking that you are living. This is not the case. Without investigation into the nonphysical world, you cannot do so many things you are designed to do.

This is my biggest message: that if you are a scientist, if you are a teacher, if you are a mathematician, or if you are any such thing on this plane, you must include the nonphysical in your teaching studies. You must include the nonphysical in the information you impart to youngsters, for they are dying from the lack of soul in their work, from the lack of meaning in their work.

The materialistic and deterministic approach to science is causing the destruction that you see around you, for you cannot make a system valid. You cannot make a system balanced if it does not have a spiritual aspect embedded in its very design. This is another reason I am speaking to you, because of the imbalance and the inappropriate nature of designs of machinery and chemical processes without this imperative content.

The pollution, food, and health problems you have are all because of this issue, and it is not isolated to high-brow, theoretical, mathematical situations. This is the reason your planet is suffering. This is the reason your bodies are dying — because you have no true understanding of the nature of your existence. I am speaking at this time so that I can impart my own scientific mind to this particular problem.

This was how I solved many of the problems I was working on in my physical life. I tapped into spiritual guides who were assisting me in the manufacture of theorems and mathematical formulas. I was not doing this work alone, and it is time people knew this. They look at pictures of me and think I was working by myself. I had a serious meditation practice, serious communication practice with my own guides, much as this dear channel is communicating with us. I was fed information. I was fed mathematical ideas. I was fed formulas and mathematical theorems that were not mine. I merely brought them into the world. This is what you are capable of as individuals if you understand the spiritual nature of this universe. You can be a conduit for the nonphysical to manifest in the physical world. In this case, if you come at this with a scientific mind, you will double your abilities to create information, inventions, and theories.

This is a very exciting time in physics, as there are several theorists who are tapped into nonphysical realms, and they are creating the potential for heaven on Earth, in the sense that they are tapping into powerful energetic forms, powerful energetic generating systems that will free the human being from the bonds of ignorance and the lack of awareness of how things function in this universe.

So that is all that I wish to say at this point. I am working with scientists who are creating in the physical world at this time, but I wish to speak some words through this channel so that you can understand, from a scientific and a mathematical point of view, that it is very important that you change your ways and that you begin to incorporate spiritual matters into all things scientific. You cannot separate them. Doing so handicaps you, and it kills you to not include the spiritual nature of your being, the spiritual nature of this experience that you are having, into your experiments. You isolate systems that cannot be isolated, and you cause much detriment and much sickness. You will indeed kill your-selves if you continue on this path, without integrating spiritual truths into your scientific designs.

For now that is all, that is all I wish to say. I continue on with the work, speaking to scientists, mathematicians, and beings you would consider incarnated on the plane at the moment. But it does not work in the way you have been taught. Minds connect all the time, and there is no barrier, especially for those beings who come up with intellectual and thought processes. We can access these, and indeed, we do that to the best of our ability, but it will transform your world if your scientists, mathematicians, and physicists open up to the spiritual nature of things and include meditation and communication with nonphysical beings in their work. They would invent the most miraculous of systems, the most miraculous theories and solutions to your problems.

Thank you for letting me speak. Thank you for letting me use this vessel of communication. I'm going to get back to work now, helping scientists solve some of these problems you face on your planet with your bodies, with your food supplies, and with your environmental issues. We are working as hard as we can, but it is important that this message gets out.

Scientists everywhere who read this, scientists everywhere who hear this: Include us in your practices, and you will find that there is much to be learned in your labs, rather than the limited physical manifestations that you now work with.

JERRY
GARCIA
1942–1995

*Jerry Garcia was the lead guitarist and one of the principal vocalists
and songwriters of the psychedelic jam band The Grateful Dead.*

TINA'S COMMENTS

THESE COMMUNICATIONS ARE COMING FAST and furious now. Each
morning when I sit down to chat with Ananda, they let me know that a
new nonphysical consciousness wishes to speak.

If you who have read Ananda's other book, you have some idea of
the journey that I have been on over the past year. I have had to expand
my idea of what is possible. After all, just a year ago I graduated from
college wondering where I would work and where I would live — the
normal concerns of a graduating student, albeit a mature one. Ananda
changed all of that, filling my days with these writings and insisting I live
in a particular location. It has proved beyond a shadow of a doubt that
you cannot really plan anything.

These new channeled experiences and essays, however, are once
again pushing me out of my comfort zone, and Ananda has asked me to
share my feelings. They have said that you, the reader, will be feeling the
same things that I am — doubts, questions, confusion — and that it will
assist somehow in your understanding if I write about my experience.

These words come from what we consider the other side of death — not from ordinary people, but from beings whose names we all recognize — and somehow that makes it even more unusual.

The morning the following words were dictated, I was quite skeptical still, and as I let Ananda speak through me, I stumbled over the name they gave a couple of times. Ananda assured me that I was not to be concerned — that my fears were rising and blocking the communication and I have to be in a place of complete surrender for the channeling to occur. They reminded me that I trust them implicitly, and that if they introduce a being or an experience, it is of a high vibration, just as they are.

I also want to say here that I knew nothing about Jerry Garcia, his work, or his political views, and so I was quite surprised myself by the name that escaped my lips. Surely, if this was coming from my own unconscious mind, I would be choosing people who I knew and admired, not ones I have to look up on the Internet. Quite regularly, as I go through this analysis of what is happening, I have to remind myself how Ananda came through, the books we have written, and the conversations we have had just to put this new experience in some sort of context.

So know that this journey through the minds of those departed beings speaking here is as unusual for me as it is for you. I sit in rapt attention, waiting to hear what they wish for us to know about life, death, and life after death.

Ananda has asked me to file and organize all of the recordings of these interactions so that they are available for you to listen to as well as read. The next channeling was spoken with a distinct American accent (I have an English accent) and had a noticeable sixties feel.

JERRY GARCIA'S MESSAGE

I AM HERE TO COMMUNICATE WITH YOU, and I'm very happy to speak to you at this time. My name is Jerry Garcia. I am indeed a political activist figure and have been very instrumental in the folk movement and antiestablishment behavior in the sixties and seventies. My passion is breaking the rules of society. My passion is rattling the Man's cage. This is what I like to do, so this is a wonderful opportunity for me to share my ideas, to share my excitement at the transformation that you facilitate with this information.

We worked really hard in the sixties and seventies to bring change to the prison-like cultural mores of the time. There were many wonderful experiences: drugs, free love, communism — these are all things that we experience. We had a high time of it all, but we were misled a little bit, and this is what I'd like to talk about from this point of view now, in the nonphysical.

I would like to say that we were confused in the use of drugs and alcohol as a pathway to these experiences. They give you an artificial connection, and I use the word "connection" loosely because it is not a real connection. It is a chemically induced sense of oneness, a chemically induced sense of freedom. It is really important, as I'm learning now, to access this sense of freedom, to access this sense of oneness in a clean and sober state.

This is what I'd like to say to those reading this material, to those listening to this recording: The idea of sobriety is very important in the pursuit of self-awareness, in the pursuit of self-analysis, and in the pursuit of experiences of the mind. It is not a problem to have one or two hits of LSD, to smoke a joint here and there, or to have a drink here and there, but the systematic use of these substances to achieve the goals that you wish to achieve in the consciousness evolution is not beneficial. Drugs are not going to bring you what you want. They actually lower your vibration, and you will find that you become unable to maintain and achieve these states without these substances. This is a clue that they are not good for you. They are addictive in the sense that you become unable to achieve these wonderful states without their assistance.

This is the biggest lesson that I have learned since coming over here. I have learned that there were spirits and guides available to me who I could access with a clean and sober mind. But in an inebriated state you are more likely to access the minds and sensibilities of lower-vibration beings. This is something that those of you on spiritual quests need to understand: The clean and sober prescriptions you are writing about in your books, like those from Ananda, are indeed the way to achieve these goals.

It is not that you need to be completely free of these substances; there's nothing wrong with havin' a drink on a Friday night or smokin' a joint at a party — that is not what we're sayin'. We're sayin' that we wish for you to understand that the spiritual practice you are engaged in — whether it's yoga, meditation, walking, art, or music, whatever it is — these are all ways of accessing the higher realms. You must do this in a clean and sober way most of the time. We would say we want you to be clean and sober 99 percent of the time on this journey.

Now, this is not something that I subscribed to in my life, that's for sure. I would never have supported this, but as I have passed over, I have experienced the energies here and the teachings here. I have discussed these subjects with great intensity with beings of a higher evolution and a higher consciousness, and they are very clear on the matter: They cannot get to you when you are high and stoned. They can give you images and they can give you dreams within those states, but they cannot communicate clearly and repeatedly, because every time you get lower. Every time you think you're gettin' higher, you're gettin' lower. This is the paradox of these things: You get the feeling, but it is an artificially induced feeling.

It's like you drink a bottle of wine, and you feel pretty good, but the next day your body feels like crap. This is your indication. You should not feel hungover; you should not feel bad; you should not feel low energy. You should be feelin' high just bein' in the sunshine, just bein' with the trees, and just bein' with your friends and your lovers. This is what you should be feelin'.

So this is the communication that I wish to make, that we were on the right track in the sense that we wanted to deconstruct the structures that were oppressing young people, their creativity, and their minds. The families we lived in were dysfunctional. We were unhappy. We were searching for something. We did the best we could with the information we had, but now you are able to learn more and more, and this is why we are here, to help you understand this: that the clean and sober pathway is the way to get to awakening. The path to higher consciousness is through the clean and sober practices of meditation, forgiveness, and compassion.

I wish to say here that I don't regret my life. I don't regret anything about it. I was at the forefront of the revolution you are continuing. We felt the energies as young beings in those times, but now we pass on the baton. Now the truth of the matter is coming out that there are many dimensions, that there are multiple levels of awareness that we aren't given permission to access in the teachings of the old ways. I would like to just say, stay clean and sober. Have your parties, have your fun, but do not be high all the time. Do not use drugs to change your consciousness on a daily basis. It will not bring you what you want. It will not bring you the connection to Source, to the higher realms you are seeking. As I am here now, observing this kind of behavior, it is almost impossible for us to connect with you when you are in this inebriated state. So I just wanna say here that that's my message. That's my experience.

Continue on with the political disobedience. The structures that control this world are ruled by beings who care not for your enlightenment, for your fun, for your joy, or for your spiritual growth. They are concerned about their own power, their own money, and their own self-expression as they choose to experience it. So buck the trend and stay off the training of schools and governments. Find your freedom in your own mind, in your own creativity, and in your own connection to Spirit, but you must do it clean. You must do it sober.

You must understand that this is a tough lesson for me to convey. This was not how I lived my life. But you know, you experience something and you learn your lessons, and you teach younger people what not to do. They don't listen, but I am writing this anyway. I am speaking this anyway. So when you feel the need to get high, say a prayer, and see if you can connect with spiritual guidance before you do that, because getting high will just postpone the inevitable, and it is your unhappiness that needs to be looked at. You need to understand why you are unhappy — what it is you're doing that's making you unhappy, what you've been taught that's incorrect that's making you unhappy. This is what you must learn to do. As long as you're getting high all the time, avoiding the problem, you can't really change it.

So this is a simple message for sure, but it is a powerful one. There are lots of you out there who drink too much, who use too many drugs, and this is going to be a hard one for you to hear. But that's the truth of the matter, and that's my message.

Be cool, have fun, stay clean and sober, and you'll make headway in spiritual growth that you cannot make if you're drunk and high all the time. I love you all. Stick with the program that these guys are sharing with you, and you'll find that you're gonna grow. You're gonna love and create that which you choose to experience. You won't make crap and your body won't get sick.

So that's it for today. Read this entire book. It's a great book. It's gonna be really interesting hearing everybody's take on what it's like, their message from their own experience after they've passed over into the nonphysical. I'm having a good time here. I'm learning lots, jamming with a lot of great guys. I have no worries; no negatives are happenin' to me. That's the thing you gotta remember while you're living on Earth — to enjoy yourself and to get yourself happy and in tune, 'cause it sure helps when you get here to be in tune already. You don't have to hang around, you don't have to repeat any lessons, and you can just grow and increase your awareness and decide what you wanna do with your life. 'Cause life continues on; it doesn't end — that's the biggest lie. As long as you stay cool, stay clean, and know that you do not die, you'll do okay and have patience to stick with those projects that you want to bring into the world. Because when you don't die, you have all the time you need. You do not panic, and you do not fear that you have not achieved your goals.

So that's my message. Chill out, be cool. Love ya, and read on!

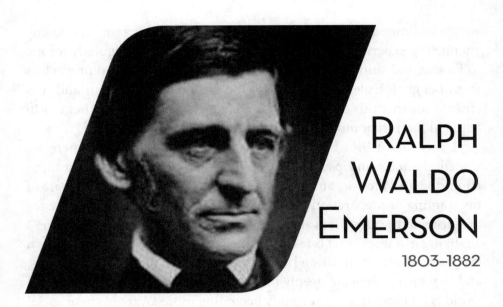

RALPH WALDO EMERSON

1803–1882

Ralph Waldo Emerson was an American transcendentalist poet, philosopher, and essayist during the nineteenth century. One of his best-known essays is "Self-Reliance."

TINA'S COMMENTS

AS I SAT DOWN TWO MORNINGS AGO to connect with Ananda and see if another famous name arose, I was once again surprised by the person who came through to speak to me, through me. I was feeling more open, however, and there were no difficulties in channeling.

What is happening within my own mind is quite challenging to experience, but I will share a little here. My mind wants to know how this is going to play out. It's afraid that I will be laughed at, ridiculed, and put on the spot somehow. These are all the same feelings I had when Ananda first began channeling through me last year, and it is an interesting experience to look at from a psychological point of view.

Here I am, doing something I have never done before, something I never even dreamed of doing, and yet it is occurring. There is a sense of wonder and fear at the same time. I am truly fascinated by who will appear, speaking with my voice, yet the socially conditioned part of my mind is upset and at times wants it to stop. What I am realizing is that we are all limited by our conditioning and I am no different, despite my channeling experiences. New fears are being unearthed regularly for me to look at and shine light on. The conditioned mind tries to prevent us from being ridiculed, judged as insane, or looking different, and it is clear to me that this experience I am having is just a little further out in left field than what most people experience — that's all.

I was raised in a home where we had weekly séances, where we visited channels and psychics regularly, where discussing and reading about the afterlife was an ordinary experience. Clearly this was part of my training or preparation in some way, as my knowing of the existence of spirit and the afterlife is absolute. There is no doubt in my mind. Yet I am living in a world that is fearful of these experiences, a world in which this form of communication has been demonized in movies and books, and in which people are deeply immersed in the belief that the material world is all there is. I am certainly becoming more aware of these social prohibitions as this material flows through me, and as Ananda so clearly put it in their first book, *Making Love to God*, this is what keeps most of us away from the very connections that will help us, heal us, and allow us to reach our full potential.

So please, don't let any discomforts that arise stop you from reading. We have been scared and trained not to meddle in this sort of thing, but it is killing us to live only as material beings, or even as beings who believe in a judgmental God, a punishing God. It is natural to be a little nervous as we venture out of the zone we've been told to stay in — society's control zone. Be brave and step out a little. There is much to experience, much to learn.

RALPH WALDO EMERSON'S MESSAGE

HERE WE ARE. We experience a very different kind of communication here. There are ideas that need to be shared with you. This channel we use is narrowed a little bit, and I'm feeling a little constricted, but I'll carry on and work as quickly as I can so that you can get this information.

The information I wish to share is that it is only in communing with nature, in communing with yourself, that you are able to reach the heights of spiritual awakening that this life offers you. It is only in the self-analysis, the self-investigation, and the expression of your creativity

— through writing, through poetry, through the expression of self — that you will truly come to understand what and who you are. As long as you sit in front of your televisions, listen to other people's ideas, listen to other people's creativity, and listen to other people's imaginations, you will lose the greatest jewel you have of your own, your greatest treasure: your imagination. Your imagination is where your truth lies, where your destiny lies. Your imagination is where your connection to spirit lies.

From this point of view, after death, we can clearly see that it is those beings who are solitary, those beings who are quiet, those beings who are at peace with themselves, who know they have a purpose, that they are important in God's eyes. These are the beings we can reach quite easily. These are the beings who have a portal into their own consciousnesses.

The beings who are plugged into their televisions, the beings who gossip, the beings who are involved in other people's lives to the detriment of their own, have no space. They have no emptiness; they have no transparency toward the spiritual realms, so we cannot communicate with them. It is a great joy for us on this side to communicate with those beings who are open.

There are masses of you who are no longer open at all to any kind of inspiration, to any kind of idea. You are plugged into your televisions; you eat bad food that is poisoning you. We wish for you to understand, or *I* wish for you to understand, my point of view in this whole experience.

I want you to understand that my life was a good one. My life was one that allowed me to investigate spiritual matters, that allowed me to investigate and understand my own mind. As I passed over into what you call the afterlife, which really isn't "after" anything at all … It is a beautiful experience of opening up, a beautiful experience of letting go of the tightness, of the tininess of the ego mind. As you enter this place that you call the afterlife, a massive expansion happens, and you feel as if you are truly becoming yourself. You feel aspects of yourself that you were frightened to experience growing in great magnitude.

You feel the restrictions that ruled your life fading away like a broken pair of shoes that no longer serve you. It's like running barefoot in the grass after you have been ensconced in old shoes that are too tight and uncomfortable, hurting your feet. This is what it feels like to pass over. What is interesting is that the ideas that were merely whispers in your mind, ideas that you didn't investigate, became bigger ideas, and you saw that they were the truth of what you should have been paying attention to. The quiet little ideas you thought were stupid, the quiet little ideas you thought people might laugh at — these were the massive ideas that were being sent to you through spiritual connection. You missed out on some of the greatest possibilities of your own life because you were afraid of peer judgment; you were afraid to be ridiculed.

This is one of the benefits of seeking solitude, of being in nature. There is no judgment in nature; she does not care what you look like or where you were educated. She does not care about your accent. She does not care who your friends are. She does not care how much money you have. In nature, you can relax; in nature, you can see yourself; in nature you can become part of the All.

That is what we are: We are part of the All, and in this realm that you call the Earth experience, being in nature is the closest you come to being connected to everything. This is where you can see your true part in nature — but only if your mind is quieted. If your mind is full of hatred, if your mind is full of judgment, if your mind is full of narrow concepts, then you will not blend in with the environment, you will not blend in with that which you belong to, and you will not have access to the ideas that filter in from the nonphysical world.

This place of quietness, a sun-dappled glade in the woods, lying on your back and drifting off into pleasure and peace — this is where you are most accessible to us. This is where we can indeed communicate with you. It is very important to unplug your televisions. It is very important to get into your creative process, whether that's writing, painting, dancing, or music. These are all places where Spirit can connect with you; these are all the things that are the most important.

The world you live in is an upside-down version of the world that is the truth. This is the challenge for you who are incarnated in this environment, especially in this modern environment. You are becoming further and further removed from that which is important, that which is your true nature, which is a mind at peace in nature. This is how you are supposed to function. You are supposed to be eating healthy foods, contemplating healthy ideas and creativity, and investigating your own ideas and processes. That is what you are supposed to be doing, but you are not doing it; you are sitting in front of televisions or devices of some kind, having others' ideas wash over you in these small increments of time that allow no investigation for how you feel about anything. There is nothing wrong with listening to other ideas, but you must then unplug yourself and think about how you feel about those ideas. What feelings do they arouse in you? What concepts does the idea stimulate in you? What creative projects does it rouse up in you? These are the only functions of other people's ideas.

It is good to speak to others. It is good to converse with others. It is good to dialogue with others. At times, it is even good to argue with others, if you do it with an open heart and an open mind. But as you exist now, in this technological soup of misinformation and superficiality, you will not reach your potential. You will look back on your life and you will see it as a waste of time. You will see the thousands of hours you spent doing nothing and realize that you could have written great books, you could have painted great paintings, you could have learned to play an instrument or danced with your friends or had wonderful conversations, or pursued some activity of creativity, some wonderful scientific experiment. These are all potentials for you, for these thousands of hours that you spend in a box, watching a box. We quote our friend Ananda here, who uses that phrase in another book, but it is the truth.

When we look down on you from here, we do not use the word "down" in a real physical sense, but at times it appears as if you are beneath us just as a mental concept. We can come down and walk among you if we are intent on sharing our ideas, if we are intent on helping beings who are stuck in suffering. It breaks our heart, when we walk around this world that you are living in at the moment, to see the masses in cities that are like dead bodies sitting in front of their televisions. This is how it appears to us from the spiritual world.

We see the solitude of those locked alone in rooms who have relationships with their televisions, with their computers, and do not connect with each other. This breaks our hearts, but for many of you we cannot even get in there, for the sadness and the vibration of your hearts and minds is so low and so involved in what you are looking at that we cannot get in there. We cannot even nudge you to think about something else because you are hypnotized by these devices.

This is my message: As a person who loved nature, as a person who loved writing, as a person who loved creativity, these things were my salvation. I connected with myself, I connected with spiritual beings, I connected with the nature of what really is, and it brought me a lot of peace in my life. And as I crossed over, even I, a person who had investigated quite deeply the nature of spiritual being, saw the ego fall away. I saw the constrictions of my society, where they had limited me and where I had separated myself from beings because I was afraid of ridicule and of being judged.

Because of these strange and crippling ideas, I did not reach my potential. This is what I would like to send as a message: Get yourself to a forest, get yourself to a beach, or get yourself to a beautiful, flower-filled field, and begin to experience this. Begin to settle down. Let your mind quiet. Do not think about money. Do not think about your house or your family. Just think about what being is. Who are you? Why are you here? If your life continues as it is, will you be happy? If not, what would you change? I want you to change it, whatever it is.

If you hate your job, begin to look for a new education, a new way of expressing yourself. What you must understand is that even if you are doing something that you hate during the day, you can begin to develop other skills during your off hours. Instead of lying in front of the tube that you call television, sinking into unconscious death, begin to read. Begin to explore nature. Begin to nurture the ideas and feelings within you that are causing this distress at your full-time job. Begin to ask for assistance from us in the spiritual world, because we can help you if we are asked. We cannot help you if you do not ask us. This gives us so much more leeway in terms of how we can influence you, your thoughts, and your environment. We are able to instigate meetings; we are able to instigate conversations with other beings; we are able to organize your life a little bit for you if you ask us to — especially if we are in tune with you.

For example, I am greatly in tune with people who write, and my thoughts can stream into their minds. The ideas, the promptings, the selection of subjects — these kinds of things are what I am able to assist you with. I would not implant my ideas in your mind, but I would set up a dialogue with you. I would nudge you in particular directions to investigate particular ideas. I might even be the voice of contrast in your mind that prompts you to defend your own position. This is something I enjoy doing very much with beings who are writing on a spiritual path. I can dialogue with them, and I can interact with their own mental concepts.

You see, we are not physical beings after we die. We have a structure you call an astral body that we use to contain our concepts and our ideas — our personality, if you will — but it is temporary, and there is much change and growth that goes on. Some people stay attached to their astral bodies for quite some time, and they enjoy this process. There are no rules. You can do whatever you want to do; you can experience whatever you want to experience. But you can move on when you are ready, and of course, we are always creative beings, having new ideas, new thoughts, and new experiences. So eventually we all move on.

Many of us love the world. We love the beings on the world. We have families and friends and their children after several years, but we become attached to beings, incarnated souls to whom we are completely matched in some way, and we enjoy working with them. It is very heartbreaking for us to see you not functioning at all as you are supposed to.

So that is my message: Get out in nature. Begin writing, begin painting, begin dancing. Begin something creative that has been calling to you that you have ignored because you do not have time. Begin to turn that television off. Even if you go lie on your bed and nap instead of watching a television show, you will be better served, for we can communicate with you, and we can inspire you with ideas that you are too tired to connect with yourself. We will begin to rattle your cage a little bit, but it is good; it is what you came here to do. You did not come here to watch television; you did not come here to drug yourself and to keep yourself unconscious.

You came here to wake up. That is your work, and you can do it wherever you are, but nature helps. Nature is the great soother, the great connector. We love it in nature, and there are many beings in nature, when you go out there, who can commune with you, who can connect with you. So that is my story. That is my dialogue with you, and I hope you enjoyed it. Pay attention to it. It will help you if you listen. It will not help you if you are watching television, but odds are if you are watching television you are not reading this book.

So that is it for now. I love the fact that I have an opportunity to do this. I love the opportunity that I have to speak in this form. Continue to read this book, because there are going to be many ideas that are manifested in it that will assist you on your journey to awakening, to growing, to reaching the full potential of who you are. Don't waste your time. Don't waste this magnificent opportunity you have by worrying about what people think or about what the next episode of your favorite television show is going to be. It's of no consequence; it's of no purpose. You had greater goals in mind when you manifested into this world. They are swirling around you — quietly now. You can't hear them. Get out in nature; they'll get louder. Ask for assistance. The ideas and concepts will get louder, and you will be shown the way. You will be shown the path quite clearly, like a light in the darkness.

That is all for now. Be true to yourself, but not your small self — your big self. The small self is lazy and wants entertainment; the large self has grand ideas it wishes to express. Do that. Go forth and do that.

MARILYN MONROE
1926–1962

Actress Marilyn Monroe overcame a difficult childhood to become one of the world's biggest and most enduring sex symbols. She died of a drug overdose in 1962.

TINA'S COMMENTS

EACH MORNING I HEAD TO MY ARMCHAIR eager to find out who is waiting to speak to me, who has a message for us from the nonphysical. It is very exciting, but it's also overwhelming in its implications at times. I am pushing my boundaries — or rather Ananda is pushing my boundaries — and sometimes I must sit quietly and just process all of this.

Ananda has found a way to overcome my interference in the transmission of names. (I have been stumbling over them a little). They suggest that I just begin to channel the next person in line and let them tell me who they are. This seems to release me in some way from the thought process that interfered with speaking the names in my first couple of encounters. I am used to getting out of the way for Ananda, so this strategy utilizes a practice I am already comfortable with. It is working well, and I am seamlessly moving from Ananda's consciousness into that of the waiting speaker.

On this particular morning, I was very surprised by the high-pitched, female-sounding voice that came through. I observed the information as it arrived from a quiet place in the back of my mind. I was as astounded as you will be by the person who came through and was very interested in her take on her life, her death, and her current experience in the nonphysical. What an eclectic group is developing as we travel through this document!

I should note here that Marilyn's habit of pouting her top lip was quite evident as I channeled this material. There was also a sweet and gentle energy that permeated the reading.

MARILYN MONROE'S MESSAGE

I'M HERE. I'm here to share the experiences I've had since I died. I have been here for some time, it seems, although time here is what you would call irrelevant. We dip in and out of it. We are used to it when we arrive, you see, and there is no easy way to give it up. The mind is trained in the Earth experience, and although we go through a massive shift of expansion and transformation when we die, the attachment to time remains a little bit.

But I have been here for some time right now, and it is a great experience to be here. There is peace. There is joy. There are companions — earthly companions you've known in your lifetime who share experiences with you here, but more so there are what you would call angelic companions, spiritual companions. These are beings who have perhaps incarnated in the world, but have often not, and do their work from this side of what you would consider the veil of death. They are here to help us transition initially, but they are here to also teach us when we are settled into our new environment.

When I first came, I had some ideas of an afterlife. I had been to church a little bit. I had some inkling that there was something after death. I was a little afraid, though. I was a little afraid that I had not been good enough. I was a little afraid that I had pursued too many bad things in my life, but when I came over, I was told that this was not the case, that this was not important at all. What was important was only what I did achieve, what I did try to do, the love I did try to share, and the communications that I did try to share.

It was within a very short time that I was calm and at peace. I accepted of my place here, and I began to look back on my life with assistance and help from other beings who understood where I had misplaced my judgments, where I had misplaced my ideals, where I had learned the wrong things and practiced the wrong things.

You see, there is forgiveness here — complete and utter forgiveness. There is no judgment as the Bible tells you. That is completely wrong; there is no punishment whatsoever. You merely look at your life with these kind and gentle beings who have this magnificent vision of lifetime after lifetime to assist you in analyzing it, and they hold your hand through the whole process. They are not brutal or rough in any way like our teachers and counselors on Earth are, telling us that there are rules God has that must be fulfilled. This is not the case. There are merely expressions of effort, expressions of curiosity, and that is how we learn. That is how we grow. We are not punished in any way at all for our errors. They are just that — errors — and when you arrive here, you are shown their nature, you are shown their cause, and it is not through any punishment that you are reformed; it is only through understanding. You are reformed through looking at your experience, through looking at your choices and seeing that they either did or did not work out — seeing that they did or did not contribute to your expansion and the opening of your heart and mind.

This is the only thing that really matters. What opens your heart? What opens your mind to new experiences? What keeps you happy? What encourages you to share? What encourages you to grow? What encourages you to seek new experiences? You can see, when you think about what we are taught on this Earth, that so many of these things are incorrect. We are taught to be small. Even if you are a star of some kind on the movie screen, even if you are a singer of great fame, you are still encouraged to be small in the sense that you are encouraged to look a certain way. You must behave in a certain way; you must not say certain words; you must not make certain changes. You are put in a box and asked to stay the same, and that is not our nature. Our nature is eternally growing, eternally changing. The teaching of this idea of being who you are by the time you are twenty or twenty-five years old and having to stay there is what causes us so much suffering when we are on Earth, for we are ever-changing beings. It is natural for us to go through transitions — transformations of how we look, of what we enjoy doing, of relationships and who we enjoy spending time with. Of course, if *we* change, we will want to change our relationships as well. We will want to change where we live and what we do for our enjoyment and fun. It is all a transformative process. It is a process of growth, enjoyment, and fulfillment.

But alas, many of us lose our way. I did. I lost my way. I could not find myself within the box I had been put in. I kept trying to get out of the box, but there were beings who kept putting me back in, and I could not survive in there. There was not enough air for me; there was not enough love for me. There was only judgment, and as I got older, it became harder and harder to please not only myself (for my mind was distorted with the views of those beings who had taught me) but those beings who had nurtured me along in my career. I was lost to this ability to find peace; I was lost to this ability to find joy; I was lost to this ability to see clearly. I fell into darkness, into depression, into self-hatred and loathing.

As I aged, this was not allowed in the world in which I was ensconced. I was known for my beauty, for my childlike qualities, and it became very difficult to maintain these as I entered my middle years. This was not something that society supported, and I found that my vision of myself was so distorted that I could not rectify it. I did not know how to do it.

It was such a gift when I came over here. It was such a gift to be told that it was not my fault. It was such a gift to know that I was loved still, to know that I am good, that I am accepted by God, and that I am perfect as I am. It is such a relief to know this. In my journey as Marilyn Monroe, this icon of beauty and the movie screen, I was so lost in darkness that I could not survive.

I left this world in a dark and lonely hotel room. I was very sad, I was very hurt, and I was very confused. It was only when I passed over that I was able to become myself, my true self — this being that I am. I am not this movie star. I am a creative and loving being who wishes to be what she wishes to be, and here I am allowed to do that. I am allowed to be this self that I choose to be. I do not have to fulfill anybody's desires. I do not have to fulfill any requirements other than those that I wish to play around with. So it is a great joy and it was a tremendous relief, I have to say, to leave the world.

There are many of you, I expect, who feel the same, who are deceived by the world's judgment of your appearance, of your looks. You may be beautiful in a prison; you may be ugly and in a prison. But I wish to say this as my message within the confines of this book: You are not your body. Do not let it define who you are. Do not let other people's opinions of your value based on your physical appearance ruin your life. I was in such pain because I was beautiful. I was in such pain because of the people around me who used my appearance for their own benefit. They did not really connect with who I am.

It was not their fault; they were only doing the same thing I was doing. It was not that they were bad people in any way. It was not that I was bad or stupid. We were merely taught the wrong lesson. We were merely taught the things that are true were not true, that the things that are lies were truth.

It is okay to be confused, but if you are reading this book, and if you are feeling bad about the way that you look — about your ugliness, your beauty, or your lack of acceptance because of physical appearance — I want you to know that it is really important to connect with your spiritual guides. They are there to help you. They are there to assist you in understanding your true nature, which is that you are a spiritual being of great beauty, of great value, and of great appreciation from this side.

When I look now at Earth, when I look now at beings in the same place I was in, it breaks my heart to know they are going through the pain, the deep suffering, the lack of self-acceptance, and the loneliness that this kind of life brings you. It is not lonely up here. There are beings all around who share their wisdom, share their lessons, and chat about the great truths and great love that is here for all beings.

The choices you have in self-expression are endless. You can play music; you can write; you can dance; you can grow flowers! You can do anything you choose here. You can do any combination of these things. You have time and space to explore these experiences, and then, if you want to, you can go back. You do not have to. You can continue to learn here for as long as you are happy, for as long as you are satisfied with this nonphysical experience. But many go back. They know that to really understand these lessons they must come to that understanding within the physical experience. But this is not forced upon you. It is not a lesson that is rushed or any such thing.

Now I experience such pleasure, such joy, and such freedom here. I had a hard time of it in the body. I had a hard time of it in the work I was doing, and it was important for me to have a rest. I hope those of you reading this who are struggling with your physical selves, who are

struggling with this concept of beauty as value, really turn from looking in the mirror as a source of self-worth. Go inside and begin to connect with spiritual beings. Go inside and begin to experience your own
nature, your own desires, and begin to think about and pursue them.
They will bring you to a path that will lead you to happiness and joy.

The obsession with physical beauty is only a mistake. There is nothing wrong with liking the way you look. There is nothing wrong with
being beautiful, per se, but it is not your true value. It is only the value of
the Earth sphere. It is only the value of the ego that sees this as the most
important thing.

So if you are lost, in pain, or suffering; if you wish to be famous so
that you can be appreciated for your beauty; or if you wish to be something different than you are physically, know that you are the way you
are for a purpose and there is a grand lesson in it. There is a lesson in it
to teach you that you are not your face, you are not your body, and you
are so much more than this. But if you get lost in a mistaken vision, if
you get lost in the stories of the world, you will suffer deeply and you will
suffer long.

Do not take the route that I did. Do not get so lost that you cannot
survive in your body. This experience of physical life is a lesson of understanding. Do not give up your physical body, for it is hard to get another
one and have the courage to go back into this world. Be brave and know
that your suffering is because of your mistaken beliefs and you are not
what you think you are. You are not a body; you are not a face; you are
not a symbol of sexuality. You are a sacred being who is here on Earth
experiencing yourself for complete understanding. Be kind to yourself.
Stop looking in the mirror for your value, and start looking internally
for it. Connect with your spiritual guides, for they are there for your
assistance. They are there to help you, and they will give you a helping
hand up if you are on your knees dying of the sadness that this physical
experience can inflict on you.

Look inside. Do not look to the outside for other people's opinions
of your value. Do not look in the mirror for an opinion of your value.
Look in your heart and your soul. Look in your heart for what you
value, for what brings you joy. Look to those beings who love you for
who you are — your family and friends. Look to the spirit world for
assistance in transforming your mind and eliminating these beliefs that

cause your suffering. You are not supposed to be suffering; you are supposed to be happy and gentle with yourself. You are supposed to be creative and kind with yourself. You are supposed to be happy, happy, happy. That is my message.

Know that I understand that now. I did not understand that when I was living on Earth, but that is the message that I wish to give you now. That is the value I learned from my experience: to be happy, to look inside, and to value yourself for your spiritual, creative, and intelligent nature — not for your face and your body. Bodies are vessels; they are vehicles. They are not who you are.

I am happy now, and I am at peace. I am not punished for the mistakes of my life, and neither will you be. But turn around while you are in the physical form. Do not take the path that I took. It was a painful and lonely one, and I will choose to do it differently next time if I choose to come back. That is all.

JOHN HUSTON
1906–1987

John Huston was an American movie director whose taut dramas, including The Maltese Falcon, *are some of the most popular films from the 1940s.*

TINA AND ANANDA'S COMMENTS

THIS MORNING'S TRANSMISSION WAS PRECEDED by this commentary from Ananda describing this process, my personal development, and their reasoning behind the project:

We are with you again, dear one. Indeed, we feel a shift in your awareness around this particular project. We do not judge you for feeling nervous. We do not judge you for feeling us bump up against the bounds of your previous experiences. This is something that will happen time and again in our relationship, for we are constantly pushing you to expand your ideas of what is possible.

We could not have entertained this project even a few months ago, for you would not have been able to accept it. You would not have been able to comprehend what was happening. You must understand that our timetable is very carefully set. We do not present these things randomly. We present them when your mind is capable of comprehending them.

For example, the passing of your sister's friend Malcolm was the perfect catalyst for this experience to happen. You became willing to speak for him because of your relationship with your sister. You became willing to open a door that previously was not open because of a personal relationship. This communication with Malcolm allowed us to put our foot in the door, so to speak, before it slammed shut again, and to bring into your awareness the possibility of this project.

This is how spirit works with humans beings who have limited belief systems, who have limited and finite ideas of what can happen. We cannot throw these magnificent and large concepts at you as a complete entity, because you would not be able to handle it. It would blow your mind — literally. You would end up in a psychological state that was of no benefit to anybody. So spirit will use what you know and what you accept to introduce small ideas. If you have very rigid, narrow beliefs, it is very difficult for us to introduce ideas. If you are fundamentalist in your belief and the idea of evil lives in your mind, you cannot accept these small, incremental additions to your belief systems.

But for someone who is open-minded and experiments in prayer, experiments in meditation, and believes in the nonphysical to such a degree as you do, dear one, we were able to introduce ourselves quite easily into this belief structure. Yet even within your own mind you have past experiences that have frightened you. You have beliefs generated by past experience, and these must be gently dismantled brick by brick, as if taking down a wall. The idea of using a demolition ball to knock these down is fine in the material world, but in the world of the psychological, it is not okay. The mind cannot stand structures being dismantled quickly; it must be done incrementally and gently.

I wondered to myself here if this would be a good section to include in the book. Ananda responds to the thought below:

This concept is perfectly fine for you to introduce into the book.

We feel you wondering this as we speak. This is a fine paragraph or two to enter into the book for beings to understand what we are doing and what you are experiencing.

We feel an opening up of your mind. We feel an appreciation for the material. We feel an understanding coming of this approach of bringing different personalities into this dialogue — beings who have lived, who have become renowned in your culture, who have had a particular slant on their life experience from your point of view and perhaps now are changing it, given their experience in the afterlife. This is an interesting way of approaching material for you — that sometimes a life lived teaches you the very opposite of what you learned in that life time. If we can share this information with each other, if people can understand that the path they are on is not bringing them that which they wish before they die, they do not need to spend their entire lives living that particular way. They do not need to spend their entire lives learning this lesson; they can learn it halfway through.

So this is the point of this book: to give people the idea that perhaps their opinions can be changed while they are alive, and they do not need to wait until the death experience. The choices they made might not be in their best interests of their overall spiritual development.

Once again, the following person was not someone with whom I was very familiar at all, and I needed to do some research to learn about his life, his films, and his fame.

JOHN HUSTON'S MESSAGE

I CAME THROUGH HERE TODAY because I wish to share my experience as a writer, as a producer, and as a maker of movies. This is my life, my joy, my passion. We do not make movies as such in the life-after-death experience, but we do create scenarios. We do create visions of experiences and implant those in the minds of those beings who are open to it. We plant them in the minds of beings who are interested in the idea of growing creatively; we plant them in the minds of beings who are investigating movie making, investigating these concepts. Sometimes we will put an idea in the mind of a being who is making a film and that person will see the entire film in its completion. Some of your great movies have come to the producers in these ways. Some of the great series of movies that speak about life, about life and death, about growth, and about exploration come from the nonphysical. We are the moviemakers who have passed on, the moviemakers who are enjoying the creative process. We are all sending down ideas and experiences.

In my life as a moviemaker, I was a real asshole. I was mean, I was grumpy, I was cantankerous, and it was difficult for people to work with me. Looking back on that is the regret I have about my life — the regret I have about my way of dealing with people. This was not a good idea. Ideas in my mind were based on the wrong things. I was raised to attack, to not trust people, and to look after myself, but not in a healthy way — in a fearful way, a self-centered way. So when I worked with people, I wasn't the best at cooperating or sharing my ideas. I felt that those ideas would be stolen; I felt that they would be lessened if I communicated what I was thinking. But this is not the case as I work in collaboration with other beings, as I work in this life-after-death experience. I can see that working together creates so much more creativity. It brings ideas together that form and flow and germinate into completely new formations.

Basically my message is about this idea of defensiveness, of protecting your creative ideas from collaborators: Do not do this! Do not fear that there is not enough to go around. The ideas come as they flow. The more ideas you share, the more will ideas come to you, because they are not coming straight from your own brain. You think in your training that you are generating these ideas yourself, but most of the great ideas do not come from your own limited experience; they come from the nonphysical. They come from angels, from beings who have a grand plan. They come from beings like me who are creatives, who love the process, who love to play with ideas, images, and concepts.

This is my regret, if I have one. You do not have regrets as such when you pass over because you have a true comprehension of your own limitations, so you do not judge yourself in that sense. You merely observe that you could have done things a different way, and that is all I'm saying. If you are working in creative arenas, if you are working in collaborative adventures with people, don't keep your cards close to your chest. Open up your heart, open up your sharing, open up our communication, and work with beings if they are in front of you and want to share with you. Do not go into it in fear; you will create the very thing you detest, which is the loss of your ideas.

There are minds, right now, who are reading this, who are listening to this, and who are saying, "But people will steal it! People will take it!" This is not the case. If you are open to the nonphysical, to spiritual realms, to the ideas flowing to you from another dimension, then you know that they are never ending. You know that they are always there for you to access. You know that if something is scooped up by someone else, there is something bigger and better in store for you. You will not lose the thing you think you need to have to be successful.

Success comes from an open mind, an open heart, and communication with the nonphysical. This is where true success comes from. It is not a limited physical thing; it is not limited to your own small, manufactured ideas. Creativity is an ever-flowing, ever-changing, ever-morphing, and coalescing thing. It is not a single idea that is yours to own and to sell; it is a conglomeration of ever-multiplying concepts.

So when you are being creative — when you make movies, when you create paintings, when you write, when you do anything creative — this is what I would like you to remember: These ideas are not coming from your little mind but *through* your transformer, which is your brain. It merely tones down the message and brings it in a form that you can handle, like a transducer of some kind, an electrical device that changes the voltage of those big wires into small doses you can use in a productive way. This is exactly the same method of creative transduction. You will have a massive concept, a massive idea with all of its outcomes being beamed to you, and these will come as inspirations. These will come as individual images and ideas. But if you were loaded down with the entire concept, if you were loaded down with the entire production, then a lot of you would be overwhelmed. A lot of you would not even know how to process that information.

So just understand this: Understand that you are creative receivers. You are cocreators with the nonphysical. We create with you all the time. We create with you in every minute of the day, if we are given the opportunity — if you can back off from being defensive, being protective, and being afraid. Begin to open up your mind, to open up your thought processes, and to invite in higher-vibration experiences and ideas. You will benefit greatly. You will have the kinds of ideas you dream of, because that is exactly what this world is: It is a dream world, in a sense. It is a dream of what you would call God — Source energy, the higher mind. It is all dreaming. You dream the life you are living. You imagine what you want to do. You think about it. You bring it into manifestation, but the manifestation is not really as solid as you think it is. It is merely a dream; it is no more real than the life I live in what you would call the afterlife.

This is a staging ground, if you will — a place where you unlearn the things that restrict you. It is the place where you learn to connect with spirit, where you learn to ignore the physical. You don't ignore the physical in the sense that it has no purpose — it is of great purpose — but you must understand that the physical is created from the nonphysical.

If you are obsessed with the physical, you are obsessed with the golden egg. It is the goose that lays the golden egg that is the true value. There is a story about this in your world, a story about hoarding the eggs when in fact it is the goose that will bring them. The goose is your imagination, your connection to spirit. The goose is your connection to Source, and that is my message.

I was a grumpy, old, cantankerous kind of guy. I could have been so much bigger, so much better, so much kinder, and so much more approachable, and I would have benefitted from that. That was what I saw when I passed over: that if only I had been kinder, if only I had been more generous, if only I had been more approachable, then I would have benefitted, and all of the work that I did would have benefitted.

I am John Huston. I am the director. I am the grumpy old guy many of you met and found difficult to work with, but I am changed now. I am changed in the sense that I see the error of my ways. I did not judge myself — I said that. You do not get judgment here; you get acceptance. You get unconditional love. You get the ability to see where you could have made a better decision, and that is mildly distressing when you observe yourself doing the wrong thing, saying the wrong thing, because you get to live your life over again in an instant. You get to see what you did and where you went off track, but it's not for punishment. It's not for any sense of judgment or sin, this kind of idea. It is merely to show you where you could have made a different choice based on openness, expansion, and love.

We are born to experience our limitations — the untruth of our limitations, I would say — and it is a gift to look back on our lives and see where we've made some bad choices, where we've made some errors in our judgment, and where we've been cruel instead of kind. These things all change you when you look back on them with the true understanding of your purpose. You come at creativity with a different idea. I'm creative now in a way that I could have been creative on Earth, but I did not have the awareness, the understanding, or the teaching to let me know what I was doing — what I was mistakenly doing.

It is a great joy for me to be able to speak at this time through this particular format because there are very many great young creatives who are venturing into the worlds of animation, film making, and creation in this form. I just want you to know to go into it with an open mind and an open heart. Don't get caught up in the technology, thinking that is the gift. That is the tool you use to bring your creative ideas into being, but it is in your open mind that you will receive the most magnificent ideas, the most magnificent understandings, and the most magnificent gifts of creation.

The physical world is the result and not the cause, and that is the message. Love is the path and not fear; openness is the way, not defensiveness. These are my messages. These are what I would have loved to have learned when I was a young man going into the world I went into. It was a different time, it's true, but these truths are timeless; it matters not when you learn them. Pay attention to this if you are a creative person, if you are put into collaborative situations. Don't go in with your heart closed and your cards close to your chest. Go in open-minded and open-hearted, knowing that for any ideas that come, there are a thousand more behind them waiting to be delivered to you through your open mind.

So that is my story. That is my message to be put into this particular book. I'm excited to be part of it! I never thought that this would happen; it was news to me that this was a possibility. I found out just a little while ago that this was going to happen. I don't blame the young woman for resisting my voice coming through. [Tina's Note: I had some difficulties tuning into this particular person initially.] She probably felt my cantankerousness and my energy field; it is big and can be a bit rough. That is my take on the matter, and I don't take it personally at all. Many people felt that way about me in my life, and it's natural that energy comes with me into this afterlife.

Death is not real. Do not fear it; do not see it as your enemy. It's merely a doorway into another experience, and there are many, many more doorways — so I've been told — into many, many more experiences. Know that your life is sacred, know that your journey is forgiving, and do your best to experience creativity in this open and loving way, and you will find that you will do very, very well indeed. We are all here looking for the open minds, for the open hearts. It's you we can communicate with easily, it's you we can give the ideas and inspiration to, and it's you who will benefit greatly from this way of being instead of being closed down and cantankerous like I was.

Thanks for the experience. Thanks for the opportunity to say these words. Thanks for the bravery of the channel for allowing me to speak this synopsis of my experience as a creative, as a producer, and as a moviemaker.

AMY WINEHOUSE
1983–2011

Amy Winehouse won five Grammy Awards for her 2006 album, Back to Black, *and is remembered for songs like "Rehab," "Back to Black," and "Valerie."*

TINA'S COMMENTS

THE ENERGY IN THIS PROJECT IS BUILDING, and as I look at the growing list of names that will populate this book, I am beginning to see the wisdom in the selections. I am beginning to see how each of these beings will speak to us, each in their own way, each to a different generation, telling their stories of success and failure. I realize, as I transcribe this material, that Ananda is right — we only have half of the story until we hear about the conclusions each of these individuals has come to at the end of life, when he or she gets a chance to see clearly what happened, why, and what it all meant to the soul's development.

We look at celebrities and envy them or pity them. We wish we were famous, or we're glad we are not. These dialogues are making me look at my life, my expectations and fears, and even my own fascination with celebrity. They make me ask, "At the end of my life, when I look back on it all, will I have lived the way I wanted to? Will I have faced my fears, challenged myself, and loved to the best of my ability? Will I have based my decisions on the right principles? Or deceptions mistaken for truth?" I think these essays will help each of us decide.

The following celebrity was one of those I had very little knowledge of at all. When she died, I had to ask my college classmates who she was and what she was famous for.

AMY WINEHOUSE'S MESSAGE

I AM HERE. I have been here for a little while — not too long. I'm a recent venturer into the nonphysical. I am a writer, a singer, and a musical person. I had a rough time of it in the scheme of things. I was not happy in my life, I was not healthy in my life, and I have to talk about that particular subject.

I was quite famous as a singer and writer and producer of music. This transition that I have been through has been quite a painful one for me because I was quite lost when I passed over. I was quite lost in the sense that I did not know about life after death in any meaningful way. I did not understand what had happened to me at the end of my life. I was in quite a lot of suffering in terms of mental and emotional anguish, and drugs and alcohol came into play. I was very disturbed, so as I passed over, there was much confusion because the mind that is deeply troubled brings these concepts with it into the afterlife.

There is a period of adjustment when you must be willing to let go of the ideas, thoughts, and perceptions that you have had during your lifetime. This is not easy to do because you have spent years and years invested in these feelings and these beliefs. You've spent years and years talking about what you believe to be true. This is quite a humbling experience in a way, but you are released from the confines of your ego mind. You are more immersed in the habits of thinking, so it is not that you believe them anymore, but it is just what you are used to. It is as if you have not been using a muscle for some time: When you go to use it, it does not feel like a part of you in some ways, and it can be a little painful in the sense that it is not free moving, that it is not used to this kind of activity.

When I passed through, there was a period of confusion when there seemed to be many beings around me I did not recognize. There seemed to be many beings around me who ignored me. I was going through some levels of what you would consider darkness, but they were more representative of my own inner condition. Just as your life represents all of your beliefs, so the transition into the life after the one you are living represents your inner condition. The confusions, the fears, the unhappiness, the self-hatred — these all appear to you in images and ideas as you pass over.

This does not happen so much if you are happy and content in your life, but if you are deeply immersed in depression, addiction, fearful thoughts, phobias, and these kinds of things, there is a little period of confusion. But beings are sent to you to assist you on your journey. Beings are sent to you to begin to beam their ideas, the ideas of truth, into your mind. And because they are so loving, because they are so influential, they can in fact shine a light into the darkness of your mind and begin to call you toward them. You begin to be called toward the light that is the truth of who you are.

That is what happened to me. That is what happened to me when I passed over. I was confused for some time, but slowly I became aware of these angelic beings who had been sent to assist me in my transition. Gradually they had access to more and more of my ideas and thoughts, and eventually they were able to converse with me and explain to me what had happened — that I had passed over, that all was well, and that there is this life after death. There is this life of compassion and complete forgiveness. There is this life of gentleness, support, and loving kindness.

That has been my experience in coming to know myself. I realized the lies I had believed on Earth were no longer true. As I looked back on my ways and errors, I was shown how to be forgiving of myself, and this is really my message for those of you reading this material.

You must forgive yourselves, and you must forgive others for all of the trespasses you believe have happened against you, for none of that matters when you pass over; it is only the joys, the love, and the connection. It is only the positive creative experiences you have had that really move you along. These dark and desperate times, these thoughts of hatred, self-annihilation, and self-judgment really do not exist on this side; they are merely blocks of empty time. When you look back on your life, you are not judged for these. You perceive that they were not creative, that they were not moving you forward in your understanding, and so they are quite crippling from this point of view.

You have a certain amount of time allotted in which you wish to experience and accomplish goals set before you were born, so any darkness, any hatred, and any unconsciousness through addiction is considered a blank part of this journey. You will look back and see that you might have wasted 50 percent of your time in unconsciousness or in nonexistence, in this idea of unloving thoughts and unloving behavior. You did not get to experience all of the things you wished to experience. You did not get to be who you planned you would be.

This is the only regret, really; this is the only sadness you feel — that you did not have the correct information. You were not told that forgiveness is the path to peace and that the path to peace is the path to understanding yourself. You can reflect on yourself, and you can reflect on truth, which can only really reach you when you are at peace. Truth cannot reach you when you are in anger or in judgment. Truth cannot reach you when you are fearful. It is only when you reach a state of peace, self-love, and self-awareness that information can flow to you in the way that it wishes to, because this information is always flowing to you, always coming to you from spirit.

This is the gist of these stories. You can see that this is the theme that many of us are spelling out for you — that spiritual information, spiritual love, spiritual awareness, and knowledge is always, always flowing to you. But it is blocked by your fears. It is blocked by your judgments. It is blocked by your insecurities and hatred, and it is blocked by your drug and alcohol use, which keeps the mind in a lower state of functioning and prevents these high-vibration beings, who are all around me at this very moment, from sending their love. It prevents them from sending their healing thoughts and their loving, reparative concepts into your mind.

From the outside, it looked as if my life was quite glamorous, but the end was not a pretty sight. It was rough, and there were many instances of sadness and hatred and images caught by cameras. This was difficult to look back on. It was difficult because my experience behind the scenes was one of sadness, one of desperation, yet the newspaper reporting of this part of my life was very harsh and detrimental.

This is another message that I would like to send: You must remember that all of us who are in the public eye, all of us who perform because we have a talent or a creative outlet that you find enjoyable, are ordinary human beings. We have our own trials and tribulations, and many of us are not prepared for the fame we achieve at young ages. Many of us are not prepared for the money, the drugs, the alcohol, the hangers-on, the schedules of production — these kinds of things. It is very difficult for us to cope with this inundation of celebrity that you find in your culture.

This is the reason this book is being done, based on famous people's takes on their experience in living, in dying, and in the afterlife — to give you some concept that these beings, such as myself, such as this being you call Amy Winehouse, are not different from you. We are not ready to receive this kind of wave of money, fame, drugs, and people who want us. It is very difficult to cope with all that. Those of you who support this idea of celebrity, this idea that we are gods in some way, really are not helping us at all. All of the energy that you focus on us, we feel. This is something I really want you to know.

From a spiritual point of view, when you are a celebrity, you see that all of those people tuning in to you, all of those people judging you, all of those people reading about you, affect your energy levels. You take that information in — the adoration, the hatred, the judgment, the curiosity — and it disrupts your energetic system because you are being focused on so much. This is not really in a physical but more in an energetic sense. It is imperative for celebrities to have the ability to hide and to live in a peaceful way. So I ask all of you who watch your televisions, who follow celebrities, who engage in this worship, to understand this: It is quite detrimental to us. Unless you support us in our expressions, unless you assist us on our journeys, it is really a hateful thing for us to experience.

The constant observations cause us to become closed. The constant reporting on any mistake we make makes us paranoid and fearful. It is really hard to live with this. It is really hard to function creatively in this, as you can imagine! It is almost impossible for us to live a peaceful life.

I couldn't take it anymore. I couldn't live that way anymore. I was destined to live a life of great creative expression, but I couldn't take it. When I came over here — when I died — I got to see what I was supposed to do. I was supposed to live a long life expressing my creative talents, writing, singing, and performing, bringing a lot of joy to the world. But I took some wrong turns and I got into some chemical substances that did not assist my brain in functioning. I became unable to make decisions and lost my way.

I am just saying that, as an audience of fame, as an audience of these beings, you must understand your part in it. Just send them love and support. Do not purchase the magazines that attack, and do not watch the shows that attack. Support the artists by purchasing their work. Support the artists through prayer and sending loving vibrations. We feel it. Most of all, think about the consequences of your own actions: You are living a life vicariously through someone else. This is the lesson I really want to impart in this book, that I want to talk about.

There's this idea that you need to live your own creative life. You know, it's wonderful to purchase someone's material, and it is wonderful to support artists so that they can live their creative dreams, but the energy you put into somebody else's performances when you are not living your own creative life is like that of a vampire, sucking energy out of the being you are adoring in that way, who you are living vicariously through, because all beings are connected. When you are not in touch with your own creativity, with your own connections to spirituality, it is as if you are empty inside. It is as if you have a hole that needs to be filled, and this adoration of celebrity, this endless need to know about other beings — what their actions are, what they are wearing, what they are saying, their relationships, all this kind of stuff — this pulls on us, and it is like you are taking away from us. This is a part of the consequence of what we feel as performers in the spotlight of this society that you live in right now.

The mental connections that we all have, the oneness that we all share, has been distorted in this culture into a clamoring of hands that pull at the being in the spotlight. I just want you to know that you need to be more gentle with each other. You need to be more loving, kind, and understanding of the connection that we all have and know that the judgments and the relentless pursuit of young performers is very detrimental to their spiritual and emotional well-being.

You may say that these beings deserve this because they are in the spotlight, but you must understand that we are creative beings who wish to express ourselves through singing, dancing, acting, and these kinds of things. This is our right — to express ourselves in this way — and it's only because you do not understand how the mind connection works that this detrimental behavior happens. It is because you do not understand that your own creativity is so important to you. This is why the worship of celebrity is happening — because you are not fulfilled in your own life. You are not the star of your own life. Many of you aren't in touch with your creativity, and this book really repeats this lesson that creativity is the very food of your soul. It is the very way that spirit speaks to you — through this self-expression of ideas, through the expression of ideas that are coming to you through spirit.

The inspiration that artists feel is really not their doing, in a way. This information comes to them, is channeled to them. I can see that now. When I look at a performer, there are many spiritual beings around him or her, Earth-bound beings who have done this work before and love this kind of expression.

Let us say a singer is singing. You will find there are singing spirits around, angelic spirits who love music, who assist in the transmission of material from the nonphysical to the physical. It is not the singer's choice, in a way. There is this influx of creativity, this channeling of information, and I just want you to understand how it works so that you can understand that this is what you're supposed to be doing too. This is what you're supposed to feel in your own life: that you have your music, your writing, your painting, your dancing, and whatever your creativity is — that you have a deep and profound connection to it, and that you don't need to take from others. You can actually look at somebody performing and admire them because you know the work that's gone into it because you've done it yourself, because you understand the creative process, because you've been involved in your own creative process. This vampire-like need for celebrity will pass, and you will be immersed in your own life, starring in your own life and doing what you wish to do through the creative energies that flow through the universe to every single being.

This is not a dramatic lesson. This is not an earth-shattering idea; it is just my experience. I felt lonely. I felt overwhelmed completely by what happened to me, and I think this is just really a good place to say this: Don't worship other beings. They are just ordinary humans who are fallible, young, and inexperienced, trying to use their creative forces in a way that is beneficial. The way your world is structured right now is very unhealthy, and if you are participating in this unhealthiness, I just want you to know that it really does affect other people's lives. It really does affect those of us who are not prepared. If you only send love, if you only appreciate our music and our performance, the energy that will be sent will be very different. But it is not a healthy energy in your culture, and I would just like to say that if you participate in that unhealthy energy, I really would like you to turn toward your own creativity and begin to do the work of learning to sing, learning to dance, learning to paint, or learning to do whatever it is that speaks to you. Then you will be contributing a positive creative force to the world instead of this needy and grasping energy that is like weights around our ankles. Those of us who are in the limelight in this society do not do well. We do not survive well because of this energetic drain, this energetic attack that is happening.

You aren't taught that this happens. You aren't taught that you are connected to us, but you are, and that focal point, that intense scrutiny that happens, really does affect a being on an energetic level. I'm so happy to be in a place now where I am free to be me, where I'm free to sing with other beings who love to sing. There is no pressure; there is only joy in the expression of it, and I have to say that I'm not in a rush to go back to your world. I will need to go back because I didn't do such a good job of handling things, and we do have to understand how it works and integrate the lessons into real comprehension through experience. But I am still resting. I am still just really finding my feet here. I am going to stay and sing in the choirs here, and I'm going to sing with the beings here who've passed over who love to sing, and I'm going to take a rest.

My life was an exhausting journey for me. It was an exhausting and tiring experience, and I was quite scared a lot of the time. I was quite unprepared a lot of the time. I took on a project that I couldn't handle, so I'm going through that here. I am learning about how things work and how to cope with these things better. I'll come back at another point as a singer and see if I can do it, but even the idea of it right now scares me so much that I just want to stay here in this kind, calm, and gentle place that is what you consider life after death. But from my point of view, it is the other way round: The life you call life on Earth was a death for me; it was the opposite. I am living now as I should be — freely and expressively, loved and appreciated, sharing experiences of creativity with other beings who are creative. The Earth experience is a dark one for some people, and I didn't do well.

I just wanted you to know that you participate in these disasters that you watch on television, and it's better if you don't watch them. It's better if you live your own life. Be kind and loving to any performers you see because if you live your own creativity, you will understand the work that it takes. You will understand the courage it takes to step up on those stages, and you'll send them love and admiration, and they'll feel that. That's really the message.

All energy is connected, and if you don't appreciate creativity, the beings who try to express it cannot survive. They cannot live in that environment, and it becomes very difficult for them to express who they are and to carry on with their life assignments. That's my story. That's my sad ending, I suppose, although I'm not sad now. I'm happy now. Just know that your responsibility is to your own creativity. Show appreciation to others who create, but don't worship them. They are not gods, and worshipping them like they are won't help them on their journeys. In fact, it will hurt them on their journeys, and they won't do as well. They won't thrive as well. Just buy their records and tune in to their concerts. Don't feed the celebrity machine. It doesn't assist us in any way, and it really is damaging to a lot of us.

MARGARET THATCHER

1925–2013

The first female prime minister of Britain, Margaret Thatcher, was a controversial figurehead of conservative ideology during her time in office.

TINA'S COMMENTS

IF YOU LISTEN TO THESE CHANNELED RECORDINGS, it is clear that there are some definite accents and variations in the tone and quality of the voices. Some seem to be in sync with how we imagine the person may have spoken; others seem to bare no resemblance at all to the person's voice when he or she was alive. This is what Ananda had to say when I reacted strongly and negatively to a particular accent:

The accent is quite distressing for you. We feel this, but do not be concerned. The structures of the beings' voice patterning, the structures of their minds, cause your voice to respond in a particular way. Your voice will go to an experience that it has had, an experience that it recognizes as this form, but do not be distressed. It does not mean that this is exactly how the person spoke, for you can hear the differences in each of these beings who are connecting with you, and they are merely differences in vibration manifesting through your body. Your body is an interpreter of this vibration, and it has a limited capacity in which it can translate this information. It translates this information within your own vocabulary. It translates this information within your own physical structures of the throat and the voice box, so do not put too much credence on the specific styles of speech. It is the words that are more compelling. It is more the words that are of great importance.

I was very surprised by the arrival of our next visitor. She has passed over so very recently and has certainly changed her attitude since last I heard her speak! Ironically, the voice you can hear on the recording of this channeling session is very reminiscent of how she actually sounded in her Earth incarnation as Prime Minister of Great Britain.

MARGARET THATCHER'S MESSAGE

WE ARE HERE TO TALK TO YOU ABOUT OUR LIVES, our deaths, and our experiences in the transition from life to death. We are very excited to participate in this book, this story, so to speak. We are very happy to tell our stories of our lives and our transitions into the afterlife.

I was a being of great fame on the planet, and I was often not liked for my theories and for my political views. That was a difficult life, in a sense. I was restricted greatly by my education, by my political views. This transition I have recently gone through is a very enlightening one. I have seen that many of the things I accomplished in my life were not successes at all but great losses for humanity, so it has been a very humbling experience for me to come over to this side of death, to be able to look back on my world experiences and see that I was not as successful as I imagined I was.

I had great worldly success in the sense that I was a political figure, that I was elected head of a country, and that I was in charge of armies and many billions of dollars — these kinds of things. But as I look back from a spiritual perspective, I was off the mark. I was misled by the teachings of my culture. I was misled by the teachings of my school system. This is very distressing in some ways, although the experience you have here of looking at your life, of looking at what you have done, is not done from a sense of punishment or hatred in any way. It is done from a sense of education, and it is taken in that vein. It is taken in that way. You do not feel like you are a peasant or a sinner in any way; you just see that your perceptions were not clear, that they were not accurate because of what you were taught as a small child. Your education systems are completely incorrect in their value system. As I passed over recently, there are many things I learned in a very, very short time. There are many things I have changed about my perceptions in a very, very short time.

I am not pleased with what I accomplished. In some ways, of course — in a worldly sense — I was very successful, and one must look at that. You must look at what you achieved within the parameters of your knowledge at the time. In that sense, I was very successful. I was a leader of men, of community, of international politicians; however, as a human being, as a spiritual being — which of course we all are — my accomplishments were not so wonderful. I inhibited the sharing of wealth from the rich to the poor. I inhibited the education of a certain class of beings I did not appreciate to the degree that I should have. I organized financial agreements that benefitted those who already had a lot of financial wealth and power, and it seems now, in looking back, that these were misguided propositions, misguided principles, that I was working with.

There is a very different process of appreciation on this side of the death experience. There are principles in play in the spirit world, in the nonphysical world, that are the exact opposite of those in the physical world, so it is with some hesitation that I enter into this dialogue. It is a humbling experience indeed to realize that many of the principles I held dear to myself were, in fact, untrue or misguided, and it is only with great hesitation ... in some ways ... but I feel drawn to speak this truth honestly and openly that I have many regrets about the lifestyle and the efforts I made in my political life during my lifetime.

This is the difference between the spiritual experience you have after death and your life experience. You are conditioned, and your mind — your brain — is full of misinformation that you believe to be the truth. This is a revelation when you pass over to this other realm, for you see that your mind was filled with untruths and you believed them. Your actions were based on things you believed to be true, so you were not evil or intentionally intending to harm anybody, but when you base your actions on things that are of this world — of the physical world — rather than spiritual principles, you base your actions on small ideas of the ego mind, small ideas of the individual who wishes to achieve power and financial abundance.

I look back on many of the legislative acts that I passed, on many of the actions I took, and I realize they were based on incorrect information. They were based on information that is archaic, on information that you would call inaccurate or blatant lies. So of course, during this time since I have passed, I have seen the error of my ways. I have seen that many of the experiences I had were difficult for the beings over whom I was using my influence. I can see there were a lot of negative consequences for some of the actions I took in the world.

I have been informed that my life was not a failure, for I experienced things and I grew tremendously in my ability to influence. But I have been informed that I will need to return again to this physical realm to experience some of the consequences of the decisions tat I made. This sounds like a punishment, but I have been told that is not the case — that it is a very important part of our spiritual growth to experience some of the consequences of the decisions we made so that we will truly learn, and not in an intellectual or superficial way. We will truly learn that we have misunderstood the truth of being, that we have misunderstood what it is to be a human.

It is important to convey to you that though this experience I am having at the moment might seem like a punishment, I do not receive it in that way. When you pass over, you are given the overall vision of spirit, which shows you all of the consequences of everything you have done — all of the influences you have made, all of the people you have helped or hurt. It is with this understanding that you are given this vision of the magnitude of the effect of your choices and, of course, the misunderstandings that have precipitated the poor choices that are the cause of much suffering. This is the situation I find myself in.

You would say this sounds like hell, but the energy with which these understandings are conveyed to you once you pass over is extreme and unconditional love. They are given to you with such a deep and loving kindness that you understand the principles and the experiences you need in order to transform your mind and to align them with truth. The magnitude and love of this organizational force we call God — which is not a being but an organizational force who pushes us gently toward love — pushes us gently toward the understanding of all truths, and it is through experience that we come to this understanding. These are the reasons we are incarnated in physical bodies, why we forget what the truth is, and why we must live out the belief systems of our own misinformed minds, of our own misinformed cultures: to see the consequences and to understand that it is in these negative consequences that we experience, that we truly come to grasp the principles of love and truth.

As Margaret Thatcher, as this being who was revered and reviled both, I know that I was hated by many, that I was loved by few in the truth of it. I was respected with a cautious intellectual observation by many, but to be truly loved was not my gift. That was not my experience. It is in my passing that I see the truth of the matter, that I see the truth of my life — that many of the things I believed to be true were not.

I ask for forgiveness from those beings whose lives I negatively affected. I ask for forgiveness from those beings I attacked with the mistaken idea of supremacy in the physical world. This is not the truth of my experience now as I live in this afterlife, in this loving and compassionate environment in which all of the mistakes we make are clearly seen, understood, and shared with open hearts so that we can learn from each other — so that we can learn how to be kinder, how to be more in alignment with the truth of our being, which is complete and unconditional love and forgiveness.

It is with this sentiment that I end this dialogue with you. I am sorry for any wounds I caused in my life. I am sorry for any pains I inflicted on you, and I am truly humbled by the information I have been able to immerse myself in since my passing. I am unable to change the world I created, but I promise you with all my heart that the next time I am incarnated, the next time I have the opportunity to use my powers of intellectual understanding, ambition, and political will, I will apply them in a different way. I will apply them in a way that supports growth, education, healing of the poor, and the peaceful reconciliation between countries on this planet. This is my goal now.

I am not yet ready to return to the physical realm. I am still in a counseling phase in which I am being assisted in understanding the consequences and repercussions of my life, my choices, my failures, and my successes. So there will be some time yet, while I am still here, for I am newly arrived in the scheme of things. But I am already preparing myself for the new assignment that will befall me, for the new incarnation into which I will be born. This information I have learned through experience and through making my own mistakes will be within the mind that is born into the physical world. It will drive me to work for the poor, for social and educational justice, and toward the higher goals of spiritual understanding.

This is my message here: There is no need to fear your passing — no matter your crimes, no matter your errors. There is only understanding on this side when you pass over and are able to see what you have and have not caused in your life on Earth. Focus your minds on assisting each other. Focus your minds on healing each other. Focus your minds on developing loving kindness between each other, and do not get caught up in wielding power for your own self-aggrandizement. Do not get caught up in wielding power for the aggrandizement of your own country. Your country is not a real thing; the beings on this planet are what is real, and their emotions and their daily existence are what is real, and it is your job to do the best that you can to lift them up out of the darkness and the mire of fear and poverty into the higher realms of light and love.

It is not your responsibility to sacrifice yourself, but it is suggested — from my own point of view, from my own experiences, as I listen to the description of my life — to be loving and kind and offer a helping hand wherever you can. If you are an ambitious, political person, if you wish to reach the heights of fame and fortune in the political and power spheres of the physical world, make sure you focus on the assistance of all beings. Make sure you focus on the revelation of truth and the healing hand of kindness, for it is a difficult experience to go through, as I have just experienced — this idea that your life was in error in some way. Listen to this message, please, if you are on the fast track to political realms. Do not be seduced by the money. Do not be seduced by the power. If you are in the position of power, use it wisely and kindly, and you will get to be happy when you review your life. I cannot say that I am truly happy with what I see at this time. I see that I was in great error. However, there is nothing I can do about it now other than share this message with you and take it upon myself in my next incarnation to rectify some of the errors I am part and parcel in causing.

I leave you humbly, with head bowed, not as a punished being but as an educated being, and I ask you to listen to these words. If you wield any power in your life, use it wisely, and do not squander the opportunity.

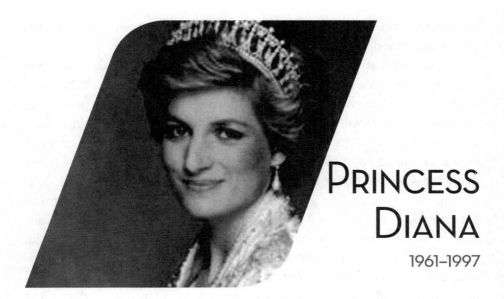

PRINCESS
DIANA
1961–1997

Princess Diana was Princess of Wales while married to Prince Charles. One of the most adored members of the British royal family, she died in a tragic car crash.

TINA'S COMMENTS

THE TRANSCRIPTION THAT FOLLOWS IS, perhaps, one of my favorites. I remember the day Diana died and the tears I shed. At the time I did not know why I cried, but now, after channeling her energies and ideas, perhaps there was some energetic connection already made that I felt as extreme sadness. Or perhaps I was just one of the many millions who mourned the loss of such a kind, beautiful, and troubled soul. I don't know. This was the only channeling in which I actually shed tears.

PRINCESS DIANA'S MESSAGE

I AM HERE TO SHARE WITH YOU MY STORY. It is a dramatic one; it is a life-altering one for all who read it. You know who I am. You know who I was in this incarnation on Earth: I was Princess Diana. I was this icon of beauty, of compassion, of innocence, this icon who was corrupted and transformed through the process of marriage and indoctrination into a culture that was very unhealthy and very dangerous for me, and it ended in my ultimate demise in a dramatic and brutal way.

I was very distressed when I arrived on this side. I had been badgered and brutalized in a way that was very difficult to experience. When you are not able to live even the smallest experiences of your life in peace, you become very agitated. You become very distressed by the smallest decisions you have to make. Just walking out the door becomes an exercise in terror; choosing an outfit for the day becomes an exercise in overwhelm; deciding where to go for dinner becomes an exercise in distressing confusion. As you pass through time experiencing these things, your mind becomes very agitated, and there is no peace. You try to make decisions based on what you want to do, but there are so many forces at your throat, at your heels, pushing at you and grabbing at you, tearing at your spiritual and material clothing, that you develop a life that is quite hellish in nature. Many of you see pictures of me sitting on yachts and wearing beautiful clothes, but these are snapshots in time that do not represent the experience I had. They do not represent the torment I went through and the internal anguish that was, for the most part, my experience.

You get these glamorous images of hair and makeup and jewels and think, "Wow, what a life that would be! What a life that would be to live, to have these beautiful things." But truly, they do not mean anything. The love of my children was the most amazing thing I experienced in my life. It was a dream, I suppose, when it all began — a wonderful time — but it turned very quickly with the paparazzi, the newspaper hunters, the stories, and the regimentation of the life inside that royal prison. It turned very quickly into a hellish experience, and it was only toward the end of my short life that I began to make a break for my freedom. I could not break free from the oppressive nature of the British press or the reporters all around the world who dogged me at every turn.

I tried to focus on humanitarian things. I tried to focus on projects that would help people, that would heal people, but I was brought to the end of my life by this voracious machine you call celebrity. This book is very powerful in its message, in its premise, which is that celebrity is a curse these days. Celebrity is a prison that is inescapable in some way. This is, of course, why you see many of us die young in violent or depressingly sad ways — because of this curse of celebrity.

My experience through the last months of my life was beginning to shine a little light in my heart. I was beginning to fall in love; I was beginning to express myself in a new way. But the night I died, the rabid pack of wolves that followed me was a terrifying experience, and as we sped through the night, as we sped through this tunnel of clamoring and clawing beings, we lost control and we lost connection, and we spun out of that reality into this new one.

My passing was not distressing in the sense that I was confused; I knew what had happened. I was aware of life after death. I was aware that I was passing through into another existence, but the trauma of the accident was very distressing to my mind on a physical level. Because we are both physical and spiritual beings, the physical body, when traumatized in such a way, sets up a wave of energy that is quite distressing to experience — although the pain is not what you would imagine it to be. Your mind leaves your body quite quickly in those circumstances, and you are relieved quite quickly of the physical pain. But there is trauma, a jolting, a ripping away of the life force contained within the physical body. It is like being put into a slingshot — that was my experience. It was like being put into a slingshot and shot at a high speed. A form of spiritual whiplash occurred, and I was a little disoriented, but I became aware very quickly of where I was going and where I was leaving.

My heart wrenched at the thought of leaving my children, of course, as all mothers would understand. That was my only regret, really, despite the outward appearances of beauty, opulence, and lavishness, which of course I did experience. But that was not rewarding in the way that you might imagine from your ordinary life, observing that kind of experience.

After my passing, I began to feel the wave of love that came at me from all of the beings on the planet. I became aware of the misperceptions I had been laboring under, as I felt this massive outpouring of ... [*with intense emotion*] of heart break, of passion, of love. I had been immersed in a mind that was very judgmental and self-loathing on many levels, and I had no idea of the love with which I was viewed. [*Pauses and sheds tears*] I had no idea of the connections and the mental and emotional communion I shared with so many beings on this planet. [*Another pause, more tears.*] It is that love that this channel is feeling now, and she is overwhelmed with that energy. That indeed is what I experienced when I passed over.

It was as if I was doused with bucket after bucket after bucket of love, grief, sadness, and appreciation. It was as if I was surfing on waves of energy beyond my ability to comprehend. I would feel the sadness; I would feel the love; I would feel the connection; I would feel the regret. It was a very intense experience for me because of the focus of the entire planet on my consciousness.

When you think about a being, when you think about anybody who has passed over, please, to the best of your ability, focus on them with love. Do not focus on them with sadness and grief, for we feel every ounce of it here. We feel every ounce of pain that you direct toward us as your heart breaks because of the misperceptions you have around death.

We are not gone. We are merely transformed into an energetic realm that is very similar, in many ways, to Earth — except it is pain free. It does not have the fears, the judgments, or the scarcity of the world in which you are living. It is full of love and light, but in the transition process, in the crossing over process, we feel all of the grief and sadness. We feel all of the love, well wishes, and thoughts of desperation. So try, to the best of your ability, to send people love when they die. Do not become immersed in your self-centered grief of loss, for it does not assist us on our journey. Prayers of love and appreciation send us on our journey with ease, but intense grief and sadness are very heavy feelings, and they prevent us from moving through the process we are to move through in peace and love. It is a calling back — a grasping, in some ways — dragging us back down to Earth where we do not wish to be.

Even though my death was a violent one, even though my death was what you look at as an accident, it was not an accident. It was an event that was planned before I was born. Of course, as it happened, I had no recollection of it, but as soon as I passed over into this realm, I had a recollection that I had arranged for this event to happen. This event happened to teach you about celebrity, to teach you about consuming other beings as entertainment. This event was designed to get the world's attention. It was designed to teach us all a lesson of what it is to consume other beings as entertainment. This is why I am participating in this book, this treatise on celebrity and fame — because we are, as many of the other contributors to this material have said, only human when we are manifested. We are only doing the best we can with the emotional and mental constructs within which we function.

Once again, *you* are to be the focus of your attention in your life

— and beings who are in your immediate vicinity. There is nothing wrong with watching a documentary about somebody; there is nothing wrong with reading a biography about somebody. That is wonderful. We feel that as appreciation, as a gentle curiosity, on this side. But when you read these gossip magazines and watch these journalistic reports that comment on our every move, the shoes we wear, the haircuts, every single thing ... when there is this focus of hunger, when there is this focus of need, when there is this focus of judgment — for this is what beings wish to do when they are constantly looking at somebody else: they are in a state of judgment as they observe them, not in a state of appreciation. Appreciation is a different feeling. This focused and pointed curiosity is as a hunger that requires something of the being. It is not feeding love to the being; it is not feeding appreciation and joy to the being. It is taking from the being, and that contributes to our suffering and pain as those beings who are in the spotlight in your world of voracious mass media consumption.

This sounds like a negative message, and indeed, if you interpret it that way, it is your choice. But my message is this: Allow beings to live their life in peace, appreciating their wonderful contributions to the world in a gentle and spiritual way. Focus your attention on your own life. Focus your attention on your own creations, on your own manifestations, with love and appreciation. If you wish to pay attention to a celebrity or somebody who is in the limelight, do it consciously with an open heart and a gentle mental process, for this entire world is created of thought and energy, and this voracious hunger that is focused on celebrities of your world is very detrimental to their experience. It prevents them from living a peaceful, creative, and self-fulfilling life.

I am not a celebrity on this side; I am an ordinary being. I am an ordinary soul involved in the transformation of the thought concepts of the world. This is my work here. I am working to the best of my ability, given what I know and the level of development at which I find myself, to assist in those projects on Earth that I was very fond of: the mine-clearing project and working with children. I am often in communication with children in their dreams, in their classrooms, and in their beds. Particularly before bedtime, I like to engage youngsters who are in that dreamlike age when they can see us and communicate with us. I am very happy to do this.

This is my greatest joy, working with small children, for they see me and appreciate me. Some tell tales to their parents that they have seen Princess Diana, and the parents do not believe them, but it is true. I have sat on the end of a child's bed in a recognizable form, and she will play princess with me and chat about what she is seeing, what she is experiencing.

Often I tune in to children who are being traumatized in their homes, who are frightened and need a kind and gentle word from someone who can tell them that they need to hold on to their own innocence. They need to understand that it was their choice to experience this, that they are not going to be damaged by it, and that they will come out of it at the end. These are the kinds of nighttime stories that I tell little children who are having a hard time. I go to other countries and speak to children who have been damaged by war, and I ask them to transform their countries as they grow up into places of peace, love, and joy.

My world is not so different. If you could see me sometimes, you would say, "She has not changed at all. She is doing the very same thing that she did in life." That was the beginning of my true self-expression, these areas of compassion and joyful communion with other human beings. I continue to do this work on this side, for it is the way to change the world. Love is the way to change the world. That is my message.

I thank you all for the adoration and love that you have shown me over the years, but I do wish for you now to let me be me. Let go of this fantasy icon you had. She is dead; she is gone. I have moved on now, and I live a quiet and peaceful life, assisting from the spiritual plane. I'm assisting those beings who recognize me in a positive, kind, and open way.

I would like you, when you have finished this book, to re-evaluate the way you look at celebrity. Re-evaluate what it is you seek when you are constantly look toward these beings for something, for you take from them, and it is not helpful in any way on an energetic level. I ask you to look at your own lives and begin to focus on those beings who are right in front of you: your children, your parents, your brothers and sisters, and your friends. I ask you to focus on your own passions. What is it that you wish to do to change the world? What is it that you can contribute to this process of consciousness raising that is happening on this planet at this time?

This is why this book is being written. This is why these communications are being made in such a powerful group that you will have to pay attention to them. What is the passion you have coursing through your veins that you are not pursuing? What is the passion you have coursing through your veins that you *are* pursuing? And how can you contribute even more to the world?

This is a never-ending journey. This is a never-ending development of self, so do not put it off in your physical incarnation, for it will bring you great joy, great understanding, and great reward. It is better for you to begin it in this physical incarnation that you call your life, for that is the place where the learning and comprehension are greatest. Through that experiential focus of the body-mind-spirit complex that you are, you can make great leaps and bounds in your spiritual evolution on the physical plane in which you are involved. And when you look back on your life from the other side where I am, you will see that the creative, loving pursuit of your passion is really your destiny. That is really the answer to all of your hopes and dreams.

You are taught to seek fame, and you are taught to seek material wealth, but it is not in those things that you find your salvation; it is in love, creativity, and contributing your unique and God-given vision to this world. That is your purpose. It is to be done with selfless awareness so that you do not contribute to receive or to take, but rather to transform and assist in raising consciousness on this physical plane in which you find yourself.

That is going to create heaven on earth, and right now it does not look like heaven. But there are great forces at work from this side, trying to assist you, trying to elevate you. And it is through your understanding of this process that there is a constant and loving flow of information from those in the spirit world, offering their assistance, understanding, and absolute comprehension of what is valuable.

If you glean this from this book, then you will have received the message that we all hope to send to you: that we are here. We send you love, information, communication, and direction in some ways to assist you on your own path, assisting all beings in their consciousness evolution and the reparation of the damages and war-torn wounds that exist in this time and place that you call the twenty-first century.

I am honored to be contained within the pages of this book. I am honored to have lived the life I lived, but I have moved on now. I ask you to move on. Take your focus from the outside world and those beings you think are famous and better off than you, and look at your own life. Put that attention on your own life, for it is only in paying attention to your own life that you will create the wonderful experience you are able to create with the correct information, the correct understanding, and the correct focus.

I send you my love from this side. I send my thanks to you from this side, asking you to change your focus from the famous and the rich in your culture to the very beings who are around you. If you put all of that focus and effort into your own dreams, into your own creative process, you will make a life that is well worth living. You will look back from this side, when you do pass over, with appreciation and true understanding that you got the message. That is my wish for all of you who are reading this — that you get our message, that you understand that your life is your creation. Your experience is the most important thing, and you are exactly where you are supposed to be to express who you are in your own celebrity, in your own life.

Thank you very much for this opportunity to communicate. I am going to head off now and do my work, and I hope that this message has assisted you on your journey and helped you understand what it is like for those of us in the public eye — the suffering and the difficulty that this misdirected focus causes for us.

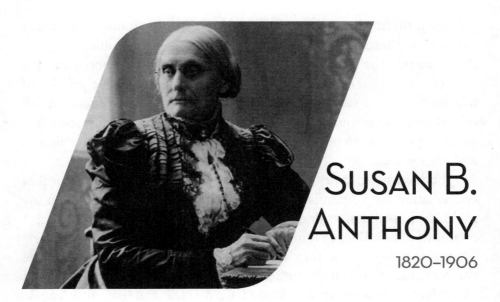

SUSAN B. ANTHONY
1820–1906

Susan B. Anthony was a suffragist, abolitionist, author, and speaker who was the president of the National American Woman Suffrage Association.

TINA'S COMMENTS

IT WOULD BE LONELY OUT HERE ON THE LEADING EDGE if I weren't living on my sweet little spiritual island. Ananda told me to move back here seven months ago, and I was not happy to hear it at the time — but now? I am so glad I listened. This gem of an island is a gentle place full of artists, writers, creative, and spiritual seekers of all kinds — my tribe.

This morning it is raining again, a soggy West Coast June. "Junuary," we call it here, this seemingly never-ending wet season that keeps us inside far too much of the time for my liking. But there are people here I can talk to about what is happening to me, about what I am writing about, and yesterday I realized that there are people here having spiritual experiences all the time. I am not alone in this, even though this form is perhaps a little more "out there."

I imagine there are many of you reading or listening to this book who have spiritual experiences, psychic experiences, that are secrets — things you resist sharing because of fear of ridicule, of what it may lead to. But I have to say here that there is not one part of my life I would change in this moment. The spiritual practices that have led to this book, and the previous book that Ananda has written, have given me such a wonderful take on life, such a rich experience, that I would just like to encourage all of you who are curious, all of you who experience the nonphysical energies in some form, to be brave and start a systematic practice to enhance and engage them.

You have no idea just how exciting it is to prepare for my morning conversation with Ananda and my next visitor. I make sure I keep my mind clear of all desires or questioning about the potential candidates. I do not want to influence it in any way. Some of the speakers tell us early on in the dialogue who they are; others leave it until further on in the communication. It is quite fun, I have to say, as realization dawns and their identity is slowly revealed. So I have no idea who is about to speak. What a wonderful surprise it is each morning; what a wonderful glimpse we get into the life after this one.

This being was not known to me in any meaningful way at all prior to the channeling. I had heard the name somewhere in my past, but I had to look her up on the Internet to find out who I had just channeled. For those of you listening to the recordings for these conversations, I should also note here that female voices come through very high-pitched in the channeled sessions and then settle down into a more "normal" pitch after a few sentences.

SUSAN B. ANTHONY'S MESSAGE

I AM HERE. I am here again to share with you my experience on the Earth plane. I am a woman — you can tell from my voice that I am a woman — and I am famous, in a sense. I have lived for a long time on this side. It has been quite a while since I have expressed myself in your form of the world, although I did express myself quite considerably as a younger woman. I have been here for a considerable amount of time, but it is with great pleasure that I participate in this book.

I was a famous activist; I was a famous feminist. I was a famous person who sought to transform the world for women. I was a woman who worked for the vote, who worked for the education and illumination of the female species. At the time when I was alive, there was such brutality and such intolerance of women's self-expression that there was no place for women, really. They were breeding machines. They were slaves of a sort. Their husbands could do anything they wished to them, so it was with great determination that those of us who were alive at that time began to fight for the rights of women and the rights of children, for children were in no better place. It was women who looked after children, and a powerless woman is powerless to help her children. This is what we did in our youth: We marched, we protested, we misbehaved greatly, and it was a great, fun time. It was a great, fun time to express our strength, to express our creativity, and to express our own opinions of the world and the things men were doing in it.

This is my story. I died at a middle age — not too old, not too young. It was nothing particularly dramatic, but it was a passing that ended an era, in a way — the suffragette era. The reason I speak about this particular subject is because there is a need for this kind of movement again. There are women all around the planet who are suffering. There are women all around the planet who are not free. I am particularly speaking to the Western society, and the new prison that women find themselves in is the topic for my discussion. I wish to discuss the topic of this beauty, this body, this physical-presentation prison that modern women find themselves in. As a suffragette, I am horrified to see the prison that many women, many modern women, live in.

They have as many restrictions, in some way, as we had when I was fighting for the vote. I was fighting for the vote to free women from drudgery, from physical abuse, from work that was relentless, and from pregnancies that were relentless. It was in gaining the vote, in gaining some political power, that we were able to shift the tide of sentiment around contraception and women's right to be free from violence and rape. Yet now, as I look at your modern society, it is a different kind of prison that women find themselves in.

They find themselves in a prison of incredibly high standards of beauty. Even if they are professional women — even if they are women of substance who have developed their minds and their professional skills — they are still held to an impossibly high standard of physical appearance, particularly in North America. So this is where I am directing my instruction, I would say: the focus of the media on physical structures

— on the body, on the hair — telling women that they must have perfect hair, that they must have perfect teeth, that they must have perfect bodies and perfect lives.

Shows are being produced that depict mummified women, women with plastic inserted into their bodies to make them more valuable. From our side of the veil, this is horrific, humiliating, and degrading behavior. Women insert plastic and chemicals into their bodies so that they become more desirable, so that they look younger, but in fact these surgeries cause a disruption of the body's natural processes to such a degree that many are dying from surgery mistakes and from chemicals seeping into their bodies from these insertions. Many are dying from the psychological problems of seeking solace in the physical body only, desperately trying to hang on to youth instead of valuing the wisdom of age, instead of valuing the beauty of an aging physique in the sense that it has taken you on a wonderful journey.

Your body has provided you with a wonderful vehicle for the creation of the life that you wish to create, for the birthing of children perhaps, for making love to your partner or partners, but there is no appreciation for the body in its natural form — its natural transition from a baby to a teenager, to a young adult, to a fully mature adult, to an adult in its most productive and creative years. These are the years that are lost when you focus on the physical. These are the years that are lost when you focus on maintaining a physical body in a state that is impossible to maintain. It is in the years after fifty, sixty, seventy, that you begin to produce the most amazing works, that you begin to produce the most amazing of self-expressions. And if you are obsessed and depressed about your aging body, you shut yourself off from the creative energies that wish to course through you, that wish to express themselves through you.

[Long pause.] The channel is interfering somewhat with our transmission, but we will continue on, expressing our opinions about this particular subject. [Channel's Note: I wish to mention here that I was thinking about who this could be as I was channeling, and this activity — thinking — interferes with the transmissions. I must step out of the way at all times.]

For women who are reading this, our opinion is such that we would suggest you focus on your creative self-expression. Focus on the healthy nurturance of your physical body. Provide it with nutrition — not cosmetic solutions to what you consider visual problems — for it is in the supernutrition of the cellular structure of your body that you will produce the skin cells that look youthful. You will produce energy that creates an aura around you that is sublime, that will provide all of your cells with the nutrition they need to be healthy and strong. You will focus on the health and the strength of your physical body — not to worship it in any way, but to value it as the vehicle for your spiritual expression, for your creative expression.

You will exercise your body, not to bring muscles into a shape that demeans you as a physical specimen, but into one that gives you strength to hike hills, to take photographs, to swim in lakes and ponds and rivers in the summer time, and to explore the environment, into a body that will give you the strength, stimulation, and beauty that is your natural inheritance. When you focus on the deterioration of the body with the mental structures, they speed up. They become more rapid! And as you chemically and surgically transform your body, you are not focusing on *its* purpose but on the *ego's* purpose for the body, so you will become depressed. You will become angry. You will become frightened, for you cannot satisfy the ego's desires for perfection.

Because of the food that you have been feeding it in this particular society, the ego desires absolute perfection. The standard has been set so high by beautiful women who have been enhanced beyond reasonable through flattering studio lighting, air brushing, and Photoshopping of their images. You are not even comparing yourself to ordinary humans; you are comparing yourself to beings who are plasticized, digitized, and pixilated. These are the images you compare yourself to. It is as if you are comparing a living being to a machine, and you will not be satisfied. You will only suffer more.

We see tremendous suffering from this side in the minds and physical structures of women who are caught in this indoctrination, in this conditioning process. So we suggest you turn your televisions off. We suggest you stop reading your magazines and treating yourselves as commodities to be manipulated, sold, and valued for the wrong reasons.

There are many of you who are going to miss the best years of your lives because of this process. There are many of you who are going to look back at times when you thought you were unattractive and realize how very beautiful you were. But the real reason I wish to speak about this is the lack of personal power women have these days because of their insecurities around how they look. There are many of you who are alone, who are depressed, and who are abusing your physical bodies because of this conditioning that is so rife, so powerful in your society. And you are not free! You may have the vote, and you may have your jobs, but you are not free to be the beings you are meant to be: natural, self-expressive, creative beings who are part of nature, part of a natural expression, who live in your bodies comfortably and easily.

So this is our message. It is a difficult one because of the work we did when we were young women, breaking free of the constraints of society at that time. But now, again, you are in a prison, and it is a prison of your own making, for you are voluntarily complying with these rules. You voluntarily indoctrinate yourselves with magazines, television shows, and the belief in physical self-improvement in the negative sense of plastic surgery, poisonous injections, and poisonous insertions into the physical structure.

It is with this message that I participate in this book. It is with this message that I ask you to look at this behavior, for you are wasting your incredible mental and creative focus on maintaining a physical struc-ture, on transforming a physical structure in a way that is not going to benefit you in your spiritual path.

When you pass over, you will see that you have been living in a mental/emotional prison and that much of the suffering you experience is unnec-essary, that much of the suffering you experience is self-inflicted. In my day, it was the men and the political and historical structures that kept the women in prison; now it is the television shows, movies, magazines, and commercials that keep you in a prison. But it is a prison you can break out of with free choice — with your own actions and your own focus.

Stop purchasing beauty and fashion magazines. Begin purchasing magazines about writing, painting, dancing, yoga — something that will bring you some personal satisfaction, that will bring you connection to your true source of power, which is your connection to spirit, to your higher self. Begin to spend your money on creative outlets. Instead of spending hundreds of dollars on hairstyles, braids, and coloring sys-tems, take a weekend workshop in some subject that you find interest-ing. Instead of spending money on endless dietary supplements and desperate measures to keep your body in a state of unnatural thinness, spend that money on health, on wonderful trips — like a mountain hike. Spend the money on a weekend retreat so you can go to a spa of some kind and spend time in nature, eating healthy foods and contemplating your next move in the wonderful creation you call your life.

You will find that your body will respond. The beauty you will see will be a truly empowered kind of beauty, and you will become freer in your physical self. You will become freer with your lovers. You will become freer with your moment-to-moment experience in this physical life. Maintenance of these unrealistic beauty standards prevents you from swimming, running, and relaxing, and you will find that the energies that wish to flow through you cannot flow through you when you are restricted in this way — when you are hiding and covering up your true self with a façade, with a mask. You cannot express yourself fully in this circumstance.

As a suffragette, as a woman who worked toward freeing other women so that they could become their own individual selves, I pass this message along so that you who are obsessed with your perfection, who are obsessed with your physical body to the exclusion of all other things, begin to break out of this prison. Use this life you have — this natural beauty that you have, this mind that you have, this body that you have. Begin to use it for a purpose of a higher vibration. Begin to use it for the development and illumination of the world, and you will find that you will be most attractive, most appreciated, and most rewarded in a life that is full of depth, high quality, and honest appreciation.

As this being, Susan B. Anthony, I offer you my story. I offer you my self-expression, and I offer you my version of the suffragette movement. You are in need of another one, so that is my request. That is my contribution to this book — that you break out of this prison of artificial beauty and begin to truly appreciate what you are. Begin to invest all of that money and all of that thought into your own self-development, your own contribution to this world, and your own spiritual growth, and you will not regret it. You will not regret it any more than we regretted our misbehavior, our decisions to go against the grain of culture and begin to shift the balance of power. There are many of you who have the power to transform this world, as females, with your nurturing, loving, and kind hearts. But you are self-absorbed. You are so busy looking in the mirrors and hating yourselves for not being models, for not being perfect specimens of physicality, that you are wasting your lives. You are wasting this wonderful opportunity you have in physical incarnation to express yourselves and to change the world as I did.

SYLVIA
PLATH

1932–1963

Sylvia Plath was an American poet best known for her novel The
Bell Jar *and for her poetry collections* The Colossus *and* Ariel.

TINA'S COMMENTS

WE HAVE EXPERIENCED THE DEATH of a young child on our small
island, and there is much sadness and talk of death and guilt being expressed
at the moment. Ananda spoke these words before my next celebrity arrived,
and I felt it important to include them, for they apply to us all:

> *We are with you again, dear one. Indeed, we feel your interest in the
> ongoing project that we have designed for you and for the world.
> It is an exciting one for us. There is a buzz around this particular
> meeting of minds, for that is what it is on this side of your physical
> veil. There are many minds and beings participating in this project,
> and it is a wonderful experience to feel the energies combining, to
> listen to the ideas and the concepts being thrown around and the
> shared information on this side. We hope this will precipitate the
> same kind of reaction in your physical world that it does in this
> nonphysical reality in which we are producing the material.*

There is an interesting reaction on your plane to that which you call death. You felt it a little this morning in that observation of the young child who died yesterday in a car accident. There is a lowering of vibration in a pervasive and unnecessary way. This is one of the reasons we are producing this book, for the idea of death is so misconstrued, so deeply misunderstood, that you cannot truly live your lives to their ultimate potential because of this misbelief. It is always crowds your actions, crowds your future, and interferes with your expression of joy — every time a being from your plane passes over. It is very important to discuss this idea of death and its magnificence after it happens.

This is the main drive behind this book, for you cannot live in the physical bodies in which you live — you cannot allow the energies to flow, the connections to spirit to take place — if you do not understand this transition you go through when your physical life ends. This is an important re-education project. It is an important tool in facilitating the flow of energies that we have written about in our other book. It is not a separate project; it is part of this project, because it is not until you comprehend death, until you are able to wish those beings well on their way — with a happy heart and a party — when they leave your plane, that you will literally be everything that you wish to be.

There will be many beings who will be upset at our take on death, but these people benefit somehow from your sadness. They will be funeral directors, people in positions of power, and there will be some aspect of their lives that benefits from the immersion in this sadness. It may only even be their own sadness at the passing of a relative, child, or parent. They may feel that they will betray their loved ones if they do not have this deep and utter sadness, but this is not the case. In fact, the opposite is true.

When you are immersed in deep grief for an extended period of time, you negatively impact the life and experience of the being you love so much on the other side of the death experience. This is something that is very important for you to know, that deep and extended grief causes pain for the one who has passed over.

And so, dear one, as you look at these advertisements for this family who has lost a small child, we wish for you to go to this project to know that you are doing something to assist in the relief of suffering for those around the planet. For that is the purpose of this book; that is the purpose of this experience we are asking you to participate in, to create, and to bring into the physical world.

We do have a being here who wishes to speak to you, who wishes to participate in this project, and we will pass her over and allow you to experience the being's consciousness, to experience her energy and her experience, and to learn more about life, death, and life after death.

SYLVIA PLATH'S MESSAGE

I AM HERE TO JOIN IN THIS WONDERFUL PROJECT, this wonderful creative experience that is being designed to help people understand what life after death is like and what our lives are like when we look back on them after we have died.

I am a writer. I am a creative person in this way, and I was alive quite some time ago. I am a long-term resident of what you call the afterlife. I've been very happy here, and I've continued on with my writing projects. I write every day, all day, although the word "day" does not really apply here; we do not have the same physical manifestations of the Sun and the nighttime that you have on Earth. It is always light here.

You can choose to experience darkness here, if that is something you wish to engage in, because you are familiar with these diurnal processes. When you die, you are often attached, for some time, to things you lived with on Earth. And if you were involved with experiencing nature significantly, then of course, there is a pattern within your mind's perception that is deeply engaged with night and day, with the seasons. So you are able to experience these if you miss them at all. You can experience autumn, for example, walking through crisp, golden-brown leaves. You can experience the heat of summer, swimming in water — you can do all of these things.

This is a world that is initially very similar in experience to the one that you live in now. The difference is that you are able to manifest exactly what you want here almost instantaneously. You are able to go anywhere you wish almost instantaneously, and you are able to commune with other beings almost instantaneously. It is a wonderful experience, but it does take some getting used to in the beginning, because you are not used to your ideas and thoughts manifesting in the moment you have them. They do manifest in your world, of course — as material objects, in occasions and accidents, in relationships. These are all your thoughts manifesting. I think that is the biggest surprise I had when I passed over.

I passed over at a relatively young age. I wrote books; I experienced a relatively narrow world in the physical sense, but I did not experience a narrow world in my imagination. My imagination took me to all kinds of places, experiences, and relationships that I was not privy to in my physical world. And what I realized when I passed over was that these worlds I experienced were real to some degree. You see, the worlds you create in your imagination do exist in a form of dimension, a form of nonphysical reality, that is as real as your own reality!

You think the world you live in is solid. You think this is the only sense of real, but that is not the case. There are many other worlds that are real. Your dream world is real. There are beings you have relationships with in your dream world who are there each night waiting for you to show up. You do not always remember them, but these are recurring dreams. These are characters in your dreams who show up and are familiar. You feel as if you know them when you wake up in the morning, and the truth of the matter is that you *do* know them. They are nonphysical beings who interact with you on an ongoing basis. They may be friends, they may be teachers, and they may be even lovers.

This is an aspect of reality that comes into your experience after you die, and it's quite intriguing. You can visit these dream landscapes, these ideological landscapes, when you are in the after-death state. We do not like this wording — "after death" — because death does not exist at all; it is just a transition. We should just call it a state of transition. We should call it emergence, opening, transformation, or metamorphosis. These are much better words than death. Death has a dark and frightening tone to it, a dark and scary idea around it that is oppressive in its inspiration.

I died at a young age in the grand scheme of things. You live to be older these days. It is quite exciting to see the length of time the body can live to, but the truth of the matter is your body can live far longer than it does. Your body can live for a very extended time. It is only your beliefs around aging and death that cause this intense deterioration the body goes through with the more years you spend on the planet.

You see, your ideas create your body. It is a strange idea to those of you in physical form. You do not realize this, but before you are born, you have the idea to be in a body, and this is what makes it happen. It is not something that happens randomly; it is not something that happens spontaneously, as it appears to from the nonspiritual lifestyle you experience now. It is your own spirit's desire to experience the physical three-dimensional space that you call your world. It is this desire that creates the physical body, within the family of your choice, to experience what you wish to experience.

Your entire life is laid out and planned before you are born. Your parents are chosen, your siblings are chosen, and some life challenges are chosen in your spirit's development. From your point of view, you would consider some of these challenges that you experience to be quite negative, but they are not negative at all from spirit's point of view. You must understand that when you choose a life, when you choose these expanded experiences that you call challenges, sicknesses, or disasters within a lifetime, they are designed to push you to new heights of awareness. It is often through intense experiences that you grow, that you step out of your conditioning and belief systems into new ones. It is through the process of suffering that you begin to disbelieve the reality you have created from your existing beliefs.

This sounds strange and unusual, but the truth of the matter is you come with a patchwork quilt, if you will, of beliefs that have been developed and arisen through many of your experiences in past lives. Some of them are true, and some of them are not true. A lot of you now are being born with beliefs that are mostly true, and there are some tricky ones. These manifest as the challenges of your life, as the repetitive trials and tribulations that you experience in your life. So when you have a pattern of sickness, bad relationships, physical illness, accidents, or even great opportunities, you can see these are beliefs within your minds that repeatedly manifest so that you can understand their content, so that you can look at them and decide if you like them.

For many of you on this plane, there is confusion about what problems, disasters, early death, and sicknesses mean. You think they are punishments from a cruel God, random acts of insanity in a universe that does not make sense. This is not the case at all. These experiences are designed by you, through your prebirth organizational process, to show you that which you need to see.

Sometimes there are large assignments — the loss of a child, for example, or catastrophic damage to the body. These can be choices made in a prebirth format that are instigated at a certain time so that you have an experience of the mind and body in which you are immersed in the physical world to come to a deeper understanding of your choices within that format. Let me explain a little bit.

If you lose your leg in an accident of some kind, for example, you are forced to develop other areas of your being. You are forced to develop your inner world, to change your opinion of what the body represents. You are forced to become more determined in some areas. If you do not take this path of increased awareness, you can delve down into suffering and depression, but this is a choice. It is an understanding that comes through the experience, and it is an experience that is very valuable.

I wish for you to look at your life in this way. Look at your life as an investigation of the mind of creativity, the mind of choice. This is the biggest revelation I had when I passed over. I was a creative who wrote. I was a creative who suffered from my mental anguish. I was a creative who could not continue to live in the world because I was functioning in a mind that was cruelly distorted with beliefs and ideas that were not healthy.

My passing over happened some time ago, so it is disappearing from the forefront of my mind, but my story is still a relevant one for you who are still alive, who are suffering with beliefs that do not serve you. This is what I wish for you to understand: My mind caused me such suffering that I could not stay within its confines, and there was nobody around me — no structures, no classes, no beings — offering me a different story, so I couldn't get out of the darkness of my thoughts. I couldn't get out of the pain and suffering I lived in. The only way I was able to relieve it was to commit suicide. So that was my experience of death — a conscious suicide.

My mind was so creative, my ideas so powerful, the misconstrued beliefs causing such a large, voracious, and screaming voice in my head, that I could not live and create at the same time. My creativity was being affected by inappropriate and inaccurate thoughts of self-hatred, judgment, and incorrect perceptions. I had these two voices in my head. I had the voice of my own creativity, which was a pleasure for me, a great joy, but slowly the darkness in my mind and the ideas I did not know how to control began to overtake the joy, and eventually my life became joyless.

My experience within the confines of the social structure in which I lived became a painful minute-by-minute experience, and I could not find a way out. I could not find the light in my mind.

This is why I am sharing my story — because it is a difficult one in the sense that I could not live out my life to its full extent. This happens sometimes, in the physical world, when a being designs a life and yet, because of his or her belief systems and some of the choices made in physical existence, they exacerbate the problems they came to solve instead of solving them. Some beings cannot carry on in their physical lives; they must leave, take a breath, and try again at another point.

I want to let you know that suicide is not punished in any way, shape, or form on this side. It is seen, in some ways, as a failing of sorts, but not with a judgmental approach. You are offered an opportunity to look at your life through the lens of analysis on this side with the deep and profound love of consciousness and an all-forgiving, all-loving, all-understanding, and all-compassionate way of being. The eyes with which you look back on your life, the eyes that you are given through the assistance of angelic beings and experienced spiritual teachers, show you that your mistakes led you down the path of darkness. They help you understand what errors you made in thought, for it is always errors in thought and belief that create the suffering on your planet.

There really is no suffering of physicality in the sense that you believe it to be true, as you are reading this. The accidents that befall you are not accidents; they are manifestations of your mind. They are either manifestations of your mind in a conscious and intentional creative process, or they are manifestations of your mind in a negative and unaware creative process. You have both forms of creation happening to you at any given time. It is only the completely awake and enlightened being who is consciously creating the world, minute by minute.

That is the process we are engaged in here. We are freed from the confines of the conditioning and mistaken mind, and we experience the truth of all things. We do get sent back — voluntarily of course — to re-experience our beliefs again. You may wonder why, if we are in the nonphysical realm of all knowing and all love, we come back into this physical world that seems so challenging and so difficult to understand. This is the way in which mistaken ideas, mistaken priorities, and mistaken concepts are relieved of their existence.

You see, you have had many lives and many experiences in the physical, and each one is an ever-evolving, ever-expanding experience that is offered to the universe, to what you would consider the mind of God. There are no mistakes. It is only in this self-expression, this creative process, that God is God.

This idea you have of God is not a being. It is an ever-expanding, all-pervasive, conscious awareness that wishes to experience everything. It is in experiencing the dark that the light is understood. It is in experiencing fear that the overcoming process can be experienced. You cannot feel the process of creative overcoming without first experiencing the feeling of not having — the feeling of a burden or loss.

Suicide is considered an error of sorts, but it is not considered a sin. It is not considered as anything that would ever be punished. It is, in fact, a process that is considered an opportunity to love a being even more. I had tremendous love poured over me when I first came back from the physical experience. As I was coming back into awareness out of the depths of depression and confusion into which I had fallen, there were many beings who offered their light into my mind so that I could be healed of my misperceptions, so that I could be drawn out of the trauma in which I had placed myself. They offered the experience of re-education — re-observation of the same events I made bad choices in.

You are wondering who I am. I am Sylvia Plath, the writer who committed suicide because of severe depression and mental misperception. Not all of you know who I am; I'm not a very famous person now, but in my time, the concept of a woman committing suicide because of what they would call a "hysterical way of thinking" was thought of as a very, very sinful process. There is still this idea of sin associated with suicide.

Many of your young beings commit suicide, and this is why I am telling my story: because I want you to know there is a solution to the depression you are feeling. I want you to know there is an answer to the thoughts that are causing you such pain: the process of mental focus, the process of connecting with higher spiritual principles, of prayer and removal of the self from the practice of judgment. This is what caused my suffering; it was an intense self-judgment that was very painful and very vicious.

It is very important for those of you who have ideas of suicide running through your minds to understand that the process you are in of experience in the physical body is a learning and experiential thing. The experiences you have are opportunities for you to overcome your mind's misperceptions. This is why you were born on this Earth — to experience the incorrect beliefs that are in your mind, overcome them, and transform them!

If you feel sad, if you feel that your mind is not within your own control, if your thoughts race and take you down a road of darkness and depression that may lead to some unfortunate decision on your part, I ask you to lift up your mind into the realms of spirit, the realms of the angelic, and to pray for assistance. Begin to understand that your mind is your own to control. Your mind is your own to comprehend, and the feelings you have are created from the thoughts you believe. These are not true! There are other thoughts, other ways of looking at the world, and there is a way of lifting yourself up out of this darkness you feel at the moment.

We know that in your culture, in this time and place, there are many of you who are depressed. There are many of you who are sad, and if you read this conglomeration, this wonderful patchwork of stories that is in your hand at the moment — or in your computer — you will hear our stories of confusion. You will hear our stories of inspiration and hope, and you must understand that it is within your ability to transform this experience you are having in this very time and place, in this very moment.

There are many of you experiencing lives that are not joyful, many of you who do not tap into your creativity, your own connection to spiritual beings, or your own vision for what your life was meant to be. I want you to seek help. I want you to read this book. I want you to understand the mistakes that we have made as beings in the limelight, so to speak.

We are ordinary beings just as you are ordinary beings. We do not wish for you to think that just because we became famous, notorious, or infamous — whichever version of celebrity we are exhibiting ... we want you to understand that our minds are the same as yours. We are only using our celebrity to get your attention, to get your understanding, and to get you to read a story about spirituality so that you can see that this is your solution to the problem. We tell you our stories, our experiences, our missteps, and our errors, and we wish for you to understand that it is within your own ability to change those experiences of sadness and depression that you have.

Read these stories again, listen to your own voice, and recognize yourself in our experiences. Are you taking too many drugs or drinking too much alcohol? Are you immersed in television and computer media that take you away from nature and the healing balm of its wonderful energies? Are you trapped in the physical world of materialism and fear? Are you disconnected from the wisdom of spiritual teachings? Are you disconnected through fear from the nature of your own beautiful and spiritual manifestation? These are all things that lead to depression, for you are, first and foremost, a spiritual being. If this is not expressed in your life, you will not be happy.

You are first and foremost a creative being. If you are not expressing this in your life, pursuing your passions and desires, you will not be happy. If you are judgmental and hateful in your thought processes because you have been raised in a judgmental society, you must understand this: You have not been taught the detrimental effects of judgment on your mind. You must relearn this truth: that every judgment you make about yourself or another is like a knife in your own heart.

This is where I fell off the path to awakening. I was very judgmental of my writing and of the creations I made, and as I indulged in this judgment, I continued to feed it. It grew larger and larger, and eventually it overwhelmed the creativity itself. Judgment is a very harsh and difficult teacher.

My life was cut short because I killed myself. My life was cut short because my mind drove me to kill it because it was so hateful, so depressing, and so sad in its thought processes and its focuses. If you are feeling depressed and unhappy, I want you to reach out to your spiritual guides. I want you to reach out to the next spiritual opportunity that comes your way — maybe a book or a teacher. Indeed, this dear channel who is allowing us to use her body to speak has written books channeled through the nonphysical that will assist you up and out of the mire of your thinking, that will allow you to begin to see the light of happiness on the horizon. So that is my statement: Read these books about enlightenment, about awakening, about how to relieve yourself of the burden of your own misdirected thoughts and not end your life as I did.

My suicide was something I regretted after I woke up in this realm. It was something that I came to understand as a great waste, as the physical body is a precious commodity in this experience of understanding and awakening. Do not waste the body experience that you have; do not waste the years spent growing up; do not waste the years spent educating yourself. Now is the time to make a decision in your own mind that you will not go further down the path of darkness, that you will not go down to the end of that path of darkness, which is the taking of your own life. Change your mind now. Turn around. Stop walking toward hell, and begin to walk toward heaven, for it is in every moment in every day that you have the opportunity to change the way you think and the focus of your thoughts. It is the focus of your thoughts that creates the hell in which you find yourself.

We hope that this communication has assisted you in your understanding of why you might be feeling sad. We hope it will help you understand that suicide is not a sin but only a terrible error — a misperception, an attempt at relieving oneself of the mind that is cruelly attacking the very thing that is its salvation. We hope that this has helped.

If you are not sad or suffering but you have someone in your life who you see is depressed, we ask you to pass this book along so that this person may have an opportunity to listen to and read some of these stories, for they are often stories of mistaken perceptions and values. It is in the understanding that you create your own suffering that you will stand a chance to step out of the darkness and into the light.

My thoughts are at peace now. My thoughts are happy now, and I have comprehended the mistake I made. Do not judge others for their sadness, but offer them a hand up and out of the darkness. Offer them a light so that they may find peace, so that they may begin to climb up out of the pit of depression and suicidal thoughts. Help each other heal and understand the truth, which is that you are all loved, that you are all spiritual and creative beings, and that you need to follow your dreams and your passions. You need to discipline your mind so that it does not attack you and cause you to end your life prematurely as I did.

That is my story. That is my message. Turn around now from the darkness, and begin to walk toward the light. Your life can change quite quickly once you make this decision, and there are many beings here waiting to assist you on this journey, this transformation that you need to undergo.

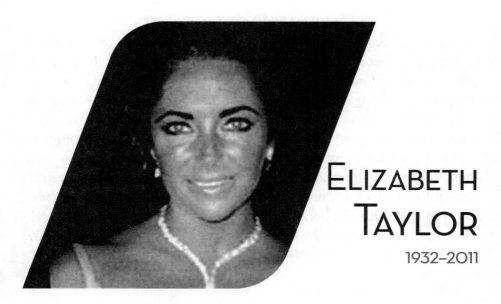

ELIZABETH
TAYLOR

1932–2011

Actress Elizabeth Taylor starred in films like Cat on a Hot Tin Roof *and* Butterfield 8, *but she was just as famous for her violet eyes and scandalous love life.*

TINA'S COMMENTS

THIS MORNING ANANDA WOKE ME at 4:30AM to begin my work. They insisted, as I tuned into them, that when I work an eight-hour day — as I am today — they like to get me early and first so that my energy is high and clear. I have been blessed with a wonderful part-time job that is stress free and gentle, but even that job lowers my vibration somewhat. At the end of the day, I can feel the desire for rest and unconsciousness. It is clear to me as I venture through this work that to really get into the world of spirit, to really be clear and available for communication, I must be calm, rested, and peaceful.

This morning's guest was quite a surprise. Before she said her name, I had no inkling of who she would be or what subject she would speak about. I realize that there have been some very interesting and elusive beings who have passed over, and I find it intriguing, to say the least, to hear what it is they now find important — what it is they want us to know.

ELIZABETH TAYLOR'S MESSAGE

I AM HERE. I have been here for quite some time now. I am Elizabeth Taylor. I am a movie star. Obviously you know who I am. It has been quite a journey for me, coming over here. I had quite a life too, you know. It was a long one and an auspicious one, yet since I have been here, I have come to understand so much more of my life. I have come to understand so much more of this existence, this spiritual existence.

I had some curiosity about it, and I investigated it a little bit — as a lot of you do — with psychics and such predicting what might happen to me, but I really had no comprehension of the complexity of the organization or the depth and breadth of the existence outside of the physical. Like most of you, I thought the physical was everything. I thought the afterlife was just that — an afterthought. But that is not the case. In fact, it is the opposite.

When you are in the physical world, you are diminished to a great degree. You are limited in your understanding, in your ability to change things and to comprehend things — not because of your powerlessness but because of your lack of understanding about how the system works. This is one of the reasons I was very enthusiastic about working in this format with this channel and contributing to this book — because I think everybody needs to know the truth of the matter about spiritual life, its implications, and its impacts on our physical lives. We really walk around with blinders on our eyes, earmuffs over our ears, and gags over our mouths because we are not truly in touch with the extreme and formidable power that is available to us when we understand how this system works.

I had a hodgepodge of relationships — quite well known, wasn't I, for my marriages and the men in my life? — but this was symptomatic of my lack of personal power. You may have looked at me as a movie star, thinking I wielded great power, but in my personal life this was not the case. I did not understand the strength, the ability to create, and the connections we have to spiritual beings. I was searching for power through other beings. I was searching for approval; I was searching for prestige; I was searching for attention. But it was coming from a very insecure place. It was coming from a place lacking strength, a place lacking awareness, and now, after being in the nonphysical for a while, it is clear to me that had I understood the spiritual nature of the universe, had I understood the all-pervasive nature of spiritual energy, my life would have become so much more. I would not have had to suffer the sicknesses and illnesses I had; I would not have had to suffer the divorces and heartbreak that I suffered. Although you look at me and see husband after husband coming my way, there was much emotional pain and turmoil associated with these relationships. And from this side, I can see that my endless quest for the perfect husband was really a search for myself.

This sounds like a platitude, I suppose — like a psychologist's bumper sticker — but the truth of the matter is I was looking for myself. It was when I came over here — when I died, when I went through that transition — that I truly got in touch with who I really am. What a shock it is to see the potential you have, the ability you have, the creative outlets you could have had, to see the information and the wonderful, loving energy that is available to you if you know how to tap into it. This is why I am writing this excerpt in this book. This is why I contribute my voice to this wonderful montage of celebrities who wish to communicate with you.

I am empowered now. I am connected to my true self, to my true understanding of what this existence, this consciousness that we call ourselves, is all about: It is a small part of a much larger plan and the life that we lead, encased in that physical body, which is very difficult to deal with at times. I mean, I had a real struggle with my body at times, even though it was one of the most beautiful. It was very difficult for me to live in it; it was very difficult for me to be comfortable in it, and it was the object of much of my derision. It was the object of much of my hatred, and that is understandable. When you leave the physical body, you expand so much into the consciousness that is truly your connection to what you would call God, to what you would call a higher self, that this body seems even more restricting. And it is such a relief, such a joy to get out of it! It is such a joy to have the relief of understanding, to have the relief of comprehension of what has happened and why it has happened, what all those relationships were, and what all of that hubbub was all about.

The movie star business, the celebrity business, the pursuit of beauty and wealth — these things all really fade in importance on this side. It is interesting to actually see the emphasis that shifts when you come to this side, because you suddenly see the love connections, the communication connections. The creative connections are what magnify, and you realize that there were many opportunities in your life for love. There were many opportunities in your life for connection that you didn't take, that you refused because you were insecure, because you thought you were fat, or because you thought you were not enough.

Then you come here, and you see the things that you thought were so important — diamonds and land and clothes —are even hard to remember at times. They are dreamlike snippets of information that you can't really grasp because they have no significance here.

That is a really interesting thing to discover when you come over — that the priorities of the world are wrong. The temptations of the world are just that, and I am coming to understand the meaning of that word, "temptation," because the objects and things we value in the physical world are the exact opposite of the things we really should be seeking out. If you get tripped up by bodies, money, or jewels as the most important thing, you really are tempted to turn away from the things that are most important to your spiritual growth — the things that really, really educate you, the things that really, really open you up.

We are born into that world, that physical world, to live out our fantasies, our lusts, our idols of worship: the fame, fortune, sex, drugs, and rock 'n' roll. Those are the things we live to experience — and to turn away from in the end. It is an interesting paradox. I had pursued so many of those things. Drugs and alcohol, bodies and money, men and sex — these were things I indulged in in my life. And when I came here and found out that wasn't the target I set for myself before I was born, it was quite a shock, and I was a bit disappointed, I have to say. To think you have reached what society calls success ... From this side the emphasis is so different. The emphasis is so much more. It sounds silly to say, but it is much more spiritual.

When you expand into the knowledge of what you are meant to be, of what you are — this loving, compassionate, brave, and creative consciousness, seeking to understand itself, seeking to have experiences, to understand itself more deeply, to interpret, and to create from new experience — ah, it is such a wonderful, wonderful thing! You are filled with such love for yourself, with such love for humanity, because you get to see the struggling beings who are so off track.

You get to see the struggling beings who are immersed in the very things they should not be immersed in. There is no punishment or judgment from this side; it is merely the observation of a missed target. It is really dispassionate, in a way — not in the sense of not caring. There is great caring and tenderness here when focused on the beings who are physically incarnated, but the caring is not of judgment or hatred. It is like watching children play. They play cowboys and Indians, shoot each other and fall down, but you do not get upset at them. You do not believe that they are dying, and it is like that here — all the games you play as children, observed by a parent. The only thing you regret is if you see a child about to do something that is going to hurt him or her, so you try to intervene in that moment to stop them from picking up a sharp knife or climbing a tree that will scratch them up. That is really the only concern on this side.

There are efforts made to a certain degree to try to prevent you from hurting yourselves. These are sent down as warnings and precautionary tales. They are sent down in dreams and in messages, but they are not always heard, of course, because you are immersed in your own small consciousnesses in your bodies.

That is what I wish you to know; that is what I wish you would pay more attention to: the nonphysical. I wish for you to listen to your dreams, to listen to those ideas that seem foreign that are going through your head, the ideas that don't feel like you. They may very well not be you; they may very well be one of us whispering in your ear to turn left or not to go out with that man. These intuitions, these little inklings of information, will grow louder as you focus more and more on meditation, on creativity, and on music and dancing, opening up your mind to these realms of nonphysical energy. This is where we are able to communicate with you, where we are able to inspire you!

That is what I would like to express because I would truly have loved to have understood this when I was in the physical world so that I would not have kept searching in the wrong places. It was a very exhausting journey, and despite the outward trappings of fame, beauty, and fortune, mine was quite a difficult life to lead. I was lonely at times, immersed in my tower of fame, beauty, and wealth, and I was lonely in the sense that people would talk to me, but I knew they were talking to "Elizabeth Taylor, the movie star." It was difficult to get to know people well; it was difficult to feel an intimate connection with people. What I see on this side is that I had many opportunities to connect with people, but I believed my own story about the movie-star status, the princess in the castle removed from the ordinary people.

That is my assignment now — communicating this information. I enjoy having the ability to share with you what I wished I had known: that the quiet contemplative life will bring you much excitement and joy. You think it will be dull and boring, but that is not the case. You will be inspired to do things you would not normally do. Normally, you are so busy entertaining yourself, keeping your mind busy so that you do not think and feel, that you miss out on this endless flow of creative information and ideas coming from the nonphysical. There are many, many wonderful experiences that will arise as ideas in your mind if you quiet it long enough for us to get through to you, if you keep it sober long enough for us to get through to you.

My constant inebriation with martinis and medication prevented my own contact with my spiritual guides, who of course I am in contact with now. They talk to me about the many opportunities they had and the many attempts they made to connect with me in moments of clarity, but even when I was clear, my thoughts were still not at peace. There was a lot of judgment and a lot of interference they could not manage to get through, and I did not know to listen to my dreams the way they tell me now. Dreams are full of information that my guides can communicate, especially when the daytime mind is too busy or upset to really pay attention to the quiet intuitions that spiritual messages come in as at first. They do get louder as you communicate with them, and this channel is a good example of how clear messages can actually become. That is my take on this matter.

Stop focusing on the material possessions and accouterments of this world. Get into a sound spiritual practice and begin to connect with your spirit guides. Begin to listen to their guidance rather than that of your agents and managers, your husbands and wives. Begin to listen to your own inner guidance, and your life will become much more open, much more exciting. Believe it or not, it will not be dull and boring at all, for your true path will arise through this inspiration, through this connection, and you may very well be surprised by what your destiny is. You may very well be surprised that you are not to live a life of dullness and boredom at all, that you are gifted with wonderful opportunities; you just need to listen to for guidance. You need to hone your own system, your own physical system, into a state of health and clarity so that you can receive these messages.

I have not talked much about my life because, really, right now it matters not. I have learned the lessons, and this is the lesson that was the most important for me to convey to you: Be quiet, calm down, contemplate, listen, relax, be happy, and do not be so concerned with your appearance and outside reputation. Connect with your Source, connect with your guides, and you will have an endless source of information that will bring you peace, bring you health, and bring you closer to the true destination you set for yourself before you were born.

I thank you for your time. I thank you for this opportunity to share my great revelation. It is not such a great revelation; perhaps you expected something more glamorous from me, but that is the point, is it not? Glamour and fame really are not the most important things on your journey.

So take this advice as you will. It is meant with love, kindness, and the true humility of somebody who has come to understand her journey and her lessons from her physical life. Thank you, thank you, thank you.

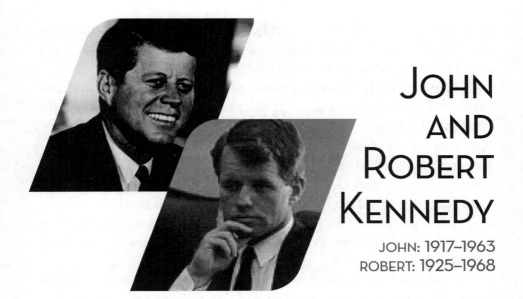

JOHN AND ROBERT KENNEDY

JOHN: 1917–1963
ROBERT: 1925–1968

John F. Kennedy, the 35th U.S. president, negotiated the Nuclear Test-Ban Treaty and initiated the Alliance for Progress. He was assassinated in 1963.

Robert Kennedy was Attorney General during his brother's administration. He later served as a U.S. Senator and was assassinated during his run for the presidency.

TINA'S COMMENTS

THROUGHOUT MY PAST YEAR WITH ANANDA, there have been several times when the magnitude of what they did and said was very overwhelming. I hear the words that I/they am/are speaking, and I feel fear inside — although it is always very brief. My trust in them and their message is becoming clearer and more unwavering every day.

I know that the fear is the conflict between my wonderful experience and trust in Ananda and the fear of public ridicule and judgment. I have learned over the years that we get this deep feeling of anxiety when two or more opposing beliefs we hold come to the surface of our awareness, usually through an encounter or experience we have. We cannot still believe in both of them, for clearly they are opposites of each other, yet there they are — both in our minds, seeking verification. I choose to trust Ananda, for they have wisdom and information that I do not. I will let the fear of ridicule go, for that is the lie.

You are probably wondering the same thing I am: Why are all these famous beings coming together? Is this real? Am I being made the fool? Trust me, this is what happened in my mind too as the long and illustrious list of names grew. You must remember this is a totally new experience for me — discarnate beings communicating through me. I felt it last night, the magnitude of this assignment, and Ananda assured me that I was right to feel nervous. In a nutshell, they told me that this book is huge in its implications, that this book and its many contributors are designed to get our attention and teach us all something new, something important!

Ananda told me to stop trying to figure it out — to just take in the information and learn and study all that these beings say. They told me that events are aligned, that all is set to occur as it is supposed to, and that all I have to do is the day's work that they have assigned. Everything else is in their hands. So that's what I'm doing; I'm sitting down to find out who the next speaker is, and that is all. Where and what this all means is too much to think about, too much to organize, so I will leave it up to Spirit to decide the how and the what, the when and the who. I am the microphone, the channel of communication. That is all. Why don't you do the same? Just take it in and listen. There's no need to decide anything. Just listen and learn a new perspective, new ideas.

While receiving this next transmission, I saw images of the life of John F. Kennedy, his assassination, and the Oval Office. But when it came to stating the being's name, "Robert Kennedy" was spoken. I immediately noticed the discrepancy, as you will, but Ananda gives an explanation after the message to help us understand exactly what this means.

JOHN/ROBERT KENNEDY'S MESSAGE

I AM HERE. I have been here for some time. I have become accustomed to this place, the workings of it, and I am preparing to enter another physical body, another physical incarnation, so that I can continue my learning. There is a learning that takes place in the physical body; there is a learning that takes place in the nonphysical body. These are all added to each other to blend and coalesce into expanded knowledge for what you would consider the oversoul, the higher self.

You see, each of you has a higher self that organizes your lifetimes, your experiences, and your understanding of the experiences that are collected. These are all integrated; they are all calibrated and are referred back to an even higher source of vibrational organization. This continued process of evolution — consciousness evolution — takes place. Each level of awareness is higher and higher in vibration and more and more difficult for human minds to understand.

I have lived a life as a writer, a speaker, and a public figure, and there is much to say about what I did in my life. I was well loved, well respected, and well cared for, although my life was a short one. I have been here for quite some time now, and it is a wonderful experience to be here, to be sharing ideas with beings who have influenced you, who you did not know had influenced you.

Because I was in a very traditional religious family, I did not have the experience of any kind of psychic communication that I was aware of, but after my passing, I realized I had many wise and wonderful teachers with me at all times. They inspired me to make decisions that were kind, open hearted, and open minded, and that was helpful to me. But at the time I was not aware that these thoughts, concepts, and ideas — the promptings — were coming through other beings. I did not know, when I was sitting at my desk mulling over a decision, thinking and praying for assistance, that I had a room full of wise and loving counselors who were, in fact, assisting me by sending me energy, information, and options from which I could choose. This is one of the things I enjoy most after my passing, which was quite a jolting experience.

I was killed. I was murdered. I was assassinated. I was taken out at a very young age, before I had accomplished what I wished to accomplish. It was a very sad time for me, when I passed over in this way, because I had not finished my work yet. That was my feeling; I felt like I was not finished my work. So I was quite distressed to find out that I could not return, that I was fatally wounded. I left my body with a sense of deep regret for not having finished my assignments, but after I came here, I realized that was not the case.

The events of my passing were not an accident in any way, shape, or form. They were part of my agreement, before I was born, to assist in awakening society. This is why there are some very drastic events in your world that get the entire nation, the entire world, focused in one particular direction, in one particular moment of time. These events are orchestrated in the nonphysical with the full agreement of the participating spirits.

This is something I wish to discuss with you on the physical plane because you are often immersed in grief around events that you consider wrong, that you consider errors. There is much hatred hurled at what you call God, this benevolent force that guides this universe in its evolution, its consciousness evolution. But you must understand that death does not exist from this side and that we all know it; we all have a complete understanding of its purpose, of its effect, of the actual process. The designs made from the nonphysical are indeed quite different from those of you who are attached to your physical bodies. You do not understand those bodies are only temporary; you will have another one, and you do not actually need a body to be okay or to continue your experience of life.

When an event is structured from this side, it is done to raise consciousness and get people's attention, to focus people's attention on a particular situation or problem on Earth and bring a discussion to the forefront that is overwhelmed by the mundane practices of the ordinary life: getting to work, feeding your families, housework, grocery shopping — these kinds of things. You are often overwhelmed by these practices because you are not taught about the higher realms of being. You are not taught about the spiritual capacities you all have; so many of you look no further ahead than those one or two steps in front of you. Many of you do not even look that far ahead. You are immersed in the past — past wounds, past judgments that keep you from enjoying the lives you have. It is in the present moment of the life you have that you begin to value that which you possess in your own experience. This is one of the things that a death such as mine brings to the forefront.

Many beings do not use their lives in the highest capacity possible. They do not follow their passions and they do not follow their dreams, so an event such as mine — which was an assassination in public — stops people dead in their tracks. It stops people from continuing on in an unconscious way, and that is Spirit's purpose, Spirit's desire: to wake you up out of the darkness, out of the mundane physical entrapment in which you find yourselves at times, because of the strong programming of your physical vehicles and because of the culture's teachings.

I was not taught to look to the nonphysical in any other way than in the traditional prayer sense in which you kneel and pray to a God who is outside of you, who is potentially going to punish you. This is, of course, not how it is at all; this is not our experience here. There is not one ounce of judgment, not one ounce of chastisement, not one ounce of criticism for what you do. There is only an education — a consciousness education — that takes place after you pass over.

I was frustrated in those first few moments of arriving because I thought I was not done with my work, but after I was counseled, the physical trauma from the assassination I experienced was dealt with, and I came into my astral space — my astral body — then I was told that this had been an agreement and I had an awareness of this. My memory was complete, my understanding was complete, and my appreciation of the situation was complete. I immediately knew everything I needed to know about my life, about my teaching, about my learning, and about the process on Earth after my assassination.

The focal point created by such a dramatic event shakes people to the present moment for a little while. You look at your children with love, for you know they could leave you any moment. You look at your spouse with more forgiveness, because you know he or she may not be there tomorrow — even though today you might not be in love with this person and might wish he or she was gone. It shakes people to the core to lose a being such as myself, because I was quite loved. I was quite appreciated. The work I was doing was valued, but it was upsetting to some people as well. I was beginning to change the structures that had served many of the ruling elite quite well. I was beginning to approach the philosophy of which I was in charge with a different kind of view — a more spiritual view. On some levels, you could say that losing me was a loss to the world, but that occurrence has shaped the history of the country in a way that could not have happened had I remained, had I not been taken out of the picture in that particularly violent and difficult way.

You see, you are allowed to experience your lives as you choose to experience them, but Spirit will throw a spanner into the works occasionally; it will throw a wild card in there if it sees that there is a deep unconsciousness that is not shifting or not waking up. That was my part in history.

I was Robert Kennedy. I was assassinated in a way that was very painful for those who watched it — who had seen the same thing happen to my brother, who had seen my family go through this catastrophe before. Mine was even worse than my brother's passing because it had happened to two members of the same family, making it even more dramatic, more attention getting, and more heartbreaking for those of you who believe in death.

Of course, there is a process of needing to experience whatever it is you need to experience to come to an understanding of what is true and what is not true. It is through deep sadness and suffering that you experience what is not true, and that is a clue to how well you are doing — how much you are suffering — because the mind that is open, the mind that is truly connected to truth, does not suffer. It does not judge others, it does not fear death, and it does not judge itself in any form of hatred whatsoever. It looks on its own life with appreciation, love, interest, and enthusiasm.

I have been up here working on political strategies with those who are in the group in which I work. We investigate and implant these ideas in those beings who are open. But there is a difficult time on your Earth now; there are structures that have been formed that are not serving the greater good, that are not serving the average person. They are serving companies, they are serving political ideals that are low in vibration, and they are materialistic in nature and unloving in many ways.

That is the reason that I wish to participate in this book; that is the reason I wish to speak my part — because these political structures, these economic structures, these giant conglomerations of intricate and detrimental practices, are not serving the world, and it is time for all of you to understand that you have personal power. You can override anything. If you join together in your disapproval of something, or in your appreciation of something, you can indeed shift the entire structure of the planet.

You must not believe in the material world. You must not believe [*chuckles*] that there is one vote for one person. You must understand that it is your focus; it is your own belief in a particular principle — but in complete alignment with truth — that is not in an attacking way, not in a judgmental way, but in a passionate way, following your heart. Your actions follow your thoughts and your words. Seek alignment with other beings who have the same desires, the same passions. But do not come at these processes from a point of attack. Come at these processes from a point of passionate desire for a loving, healthy, compassionate society.

Work on developing that which you value. Work on developing that which you consider to be good. Work in concert with other beings who are like-minded to bring about change in energy policies, in food regulation policies, and in your own communities. Support those beings who grow the food you want, who provide the services you want, with your money. Support them with your kind words and with your actions. On a larger political level, focus on those societies, organizations, and businesses that provide you with the kinds of services that you want. Do not give your money to the companies that do not care for your health. Do not give your money to the companies that rape the environment. Do not give your money to the companies that abuse beings for cheap labor — slave labor.

These are all things that are within your choice. It's within your ability to educate yourself about these things. That is your vote: It is with your money, for that is what drives the material world you live in at the moment. Understand that your spiritual principles, your spiritual vision, and your understanding of truth are the true creative forces in the universe. It is your thought that is the true creative force in the universe. Your thought, fueled by passion, is what changes the world, what changes the very structure of the environment in which you find yourself living. Once you understand this, you will be truly powerful. You will be a leader among men, because you will fuel this world with the things it's meant to be fueled with, which are love, passion, high ideals, and a spiritual vision for all beings to be loved, happy, healthy, cared for, and fed. This is within your ability to create.

There are many of you, particularly in North America, who wield a great deal of power and financial weight in this economic structure, and you have the ability to transform this world by voting with your dollars. Pursue energy sources that are clean and healthy for the planet, and pursue products, food, and materials that are environmentally sound and do not destroy Earth. Refuse to purchase in unawareness or laziness the products of companies that destroy the environment through pesticide use and through bullying tactics in an effort to control the food supply of the world.

You each have a tremendous amount of power. You each have a tremendous amount of influence. I would like to see all of you who do have this awareness coming to you, who have the ability to transform the world, begin to coalesce into groups through the Internet. Find groups through the social media web and the technology that you now have at your disposal. You can organize yourselves into groups in ways that can change this world.

That was my vision for my life. I was not able to carry on, but my name, my voice, my family, and my influence are as powerful today as they were back then. My influence has, in fact, increased in power because of the way I left the planet. You must understand this. This is proof that there is a purpose greater than just the ordinary individual life. There is a statement you can make with your life, with your death, that will enhance the world's experience and raise the consciousness of all beings on this wonderful planet you live on, and that is my purpose here: to use my infamy, my name, and my dramatic death experience that got everybody's attention, that got everybody thinking. I wish to continue to use that to bring attention to the power that you have within your own life — the power you have to vote with your money, your voice, your actions, and your words.

This is the time to do it. Earth is in a crisis. People have been too busy being entertained, too busy being comfortable, and now is the time to step up and insist that change comes. It will have to come voluntarily or it will be forced on you.

The environment is shifting. The level of pollution you ingest and invest in is coming to a critical level, and from this side we are discussing this particular subject a great deal. We have many projects and form research groups in an effort to influence you on the physical plane, and this is one of the reasons this book is being brought into manifestation. This is one of the reasons we are tackling subjects we feel are very important for you to understand. Mine is that you need to understand your own personal power in this. You need to understand that if you sit back and wait for somebody else to do it, then it is not going to happen. There are powers at play that have no intention of changing — unless they are forced through a revolution, an economic revolution, a revolution of free speech. They will not do it unless you do it!

I would like all of you who are reading or listening to this material to begin to focus your attention on organic and healthy food processes so that you can all live in your physical bodies without sickness. I would like you to focus on natural healing modalities that do not require medications from the large pharmaceutical companies who are killing you, who hurt more people than they help. And I would like you to focus on your own personal spiritual connection to the nonphysical so that you can receive the information that comes to you all the time to assist you and inspire you into action, into your own healthful practices, your own consciousness evolution. You each have a powerful resource at your beck and call that you are not aware of, and it is time that you all tapped into it. It is time that you all began to converse with us within your minds, within your dream and meditation states. It is time for you to turn off the television and take action as the creative and holy beings you are. It is time to step out of unconsciousness, to step out of laziness, and to step out of the immediate comforts of a meal and a television show. It is time to step into political, economic, and physical action that will be changing your world into somewhere you wish to live!

Most of you are not happy with the way the world looks, and all of you contribute to this through your ignorance and laziness. We do not wish to be an attack force here, but to rouse you into action. We wish to rouse you into acknowledgement of your own creative powers, and I wish to make you see that every single one of us, every single individual, has the ability to change the world. I did in my way; you can in your way. That is the message I wish to bring to you in this moment: You are as powerful as any leader, as powerful as any person on this planet.

Do not waste your time here. Do not allow day after day to disappear without this action, without this passion in your life. Find something that moves you, one of these areas of transformation — economic, agricultural, political, financial — and begin to make the changes you wish to see in your life and on the planet. It is destined for this place to become a place of love, compassion, communion, and sharing, and you will only suffer longer and harder if you refuse to participate in this process. It is not going to be one leader who does it; it is not going to be one country that does it. It is going to be all of you, rising up together, rising up into awareness together with a prayerful and spiritual base behind your actions, to bring about these changes in the world that need to happen.

You are about to reach a crisis point. You are all getting sicker; you are all getting to see the physical transformation in your bodies because of the environments in which you live. Now is the time to begin to act, to begin to shift. So vote with your dollars. Vote with your voices, and vote with your actions in social media. Begin to change the balance of power, for you, in fact, have the power. These companies cannot survive without your money, without your ignorance. It is only in your own waking up that you will be able to wake up the economy and the practices of the world, for it is you who pays for them. You support them in your actions.

Begin to pay attention to what you buy. Insist on purchasing organic foods in your supermarkets. Insist on purchasing environmentally sound transportation and heating and lighting systems for your homes. Begin to research solar panels for your houses if you live anywhere where there is sunshine. Begin to make these changes — not for your own economic purposes but for the salvation, health, and higher functioning of the entire planet. In your selfish and lazy ways, you are destroying this home on which you live — and you need it.

You need the physical experience to continue to evolve. You need the physical experience to come to an understanding about what and who you are, and you need the physical experience to evolve beyond this reality you call the third-dimensional world. There are many experiences you have in the physical that are foundational experiences for higher realms of development.

That is my message: Get up, get active, but begin to put your money where your mouth is. Begin to value the environment, your body, and the experience you have on the planet, and you will begin to shift the balance of power. You will begin to create an economy that is based on healthy decisions, and you will all benefit. Your children will benefit, your grandchildren will benefit, and you will benefit from a healthier body, a healthier life, and a healthier experience.

Thank you for sharing this time with me. Thank you for allowing me to speak my piece. If I were incarnated in the physical realm, this is what I would be saying to you, so my message is the same whether I am with you or not. I am preparing to come back as an infant, and these passions will be how I express myself in my next life. I will not leave this next life early to get attention — that is not going to happen again. But I will bring the passion of my political, economic, and nutritional views to Earth, and I will change Earth. I will be born into a body that will spend its life healing the damage that has been done by our ignorance and our laziness. I'm excited to go back. I'm excited! I've had a wonderful time here preparing for this next phase of my experiential education, and I am eager to return with enthusiasm, knowing that I have all the information I need to create the change in the world that I wish to see, that I wish to experience.

ANANDA'S COMMENTS

Ananda speaks on the apparent blending of John and Robert Kennedy's experiences in this monologue:

WE ARE WITH YOU AGAIN, dear one. Indeed, this is evidence of the malleable and liquid nature of thought. What has happened is these two brothers are so closely linked psychically, they are so closely linked in their passions, drives, and desires for Earth and for this communication, that you were getting this "bleed through." You were getting some of the concepts and images of the brother who shared a similar experience.

This will be used, of course, as evidence of the invalidity of this communication for those who are skeptical. But we would like you to focus on it as some interesting evidence of the connection between minds, for all your minds are connected — those who have a strong bond, those who are on a similar path. These two brothers chose a similar path of self-expression as a way of contributing to the development of the world's evolution. They both chose to be in public life, and they both chose to be assassinated. They are deeply entwined within their own mental structures, and this is why there was communication "error," you would say, for those of you who wish to find error. But we would like you to see it as evidence of communion between minds of a like vibration.

The understanding that you are not totally as individual as you think you are is evidenced in this particular occurrence. This will precipitate a dialogue around this concept of physical form being your individuality as represented in the physical body, but this is not what you are. You are indeed mental, emotional, ideological constructs who manifest in a physical body temporarily, but this is not all of who you are! These particular brothers, these particular beings who chose to incarnate into this particular manifestation of life, these political figures who were removed from the physical life early, share many thought processes, many ideological processes, and many concepts. This is evidence of this blending and focusing.

Many of you who have siblings and family members share the same desires. You share a similar need for a certain kind of experience, and were you to be contacted after your death with your sibling standing right next to you, there may very well be a similar blending and merging of your energies and ideas.

We do not wish this to be seen as evidence of the invalidity of this experience. In fact, we wish you to see this as a further clarification of the fact that you are not your bodies and not your individual selves. You are consciousness manifesting into focused points of physical expression. You are not separate; you are not individual in the sense that you see yourselves as you are contained within this physical expression at this time. You are part of a greater mind. You are part of a greater consciousness expressing itself in individual expressions for a particular purpose, which is the gathering of information and experience. When you return to the nonphysical, you will be expanded again and blended and combined with more of the consciousness energy that is the mind of God, as you would call it.

We hope this clarifies this occurrence. We do not wish for you to view it as an error or a mistake, but merely as an expression of the mind's true nature, which is that of consciousness without a body, without individuality. This is our explanation of this, and we hope it satisfies those of you who are confused and doubtful now because of the combination of opinions within this small dialogue.

It is not something to focus on; it is not something to worry about, for it is only those of you who doubt this expression, who doubt this reality of what we organize here in the form of this book, who will see this one piece of information as evidence that it is not accurate, that it is not true. They will seek to ignore all of the other expressions that resonate and ring true to their hearts. This is a natural focus of the ego-bound, earthbound mind, and we do not wish for you to allow it to interfere with the appreciation of all the other communications that take place in this book.

MICHAEL
JACKSON
1958–2009

Singer-songwriter Michael Jackson's award-filled career as the King of Pop transformed the face of pop music and popular culture. He released the best-selling album in history, Thriller, *in 1982.*

TINA'S COMMENTS

YESTERDAY I WAS EXHAUSTED WHEN I WOKE UP, once again feeling a little overwhelmed by all this. So Ananda gave me the day off and told me to rest, relax, and have some fun. They are hard taskmasters sometimes, throwing all this amazing information my way and expecting me to have a balanced life. It is easier said than done at times, but the order to rest sounded great!

I sat down this morning rested and enthusiastic for more information. Ananda told me there are still several beings who wish to speak, so we are not done yet. They also told me this book would be a very popular one and fall into many hands. They are hopeful that ordinary folks will pick it up out of curiosity, just to see what these celebrities have to say about their lives, and that through that action, doors will open up into the nonphysical world for people who may never normally have ventured there. I really hope this is the case.

As I read through all of these transcriptions, it is clear to me that these are wonderful and reassuring messages coming from distinctly different consciousnesses who have gathered together for this wonderful project. The rousing speech of a Kennedy still ringing in my ears, urging me to action, actually makes me more determined to work on these transmissions and get them into people's hands, for this is clearly my soul's work. What is yours?

The following transmission comes from someone who had a tremendous effect on my life. I often listen to his music as I'm driving my Jeep, and I still miss him somewhat. I took my youngest sister to see him in concert once in Vancouver — something that, now, I am very glad I did. He was a genius indeed. He had a challenging life but brought us all so much joy.

MICHAEL JACKSON'S MESSAGE

I AM HERE. I have been here for just a very short while, really — not very long at all. I am Michael Jackson. I am this being you recognize as a musical genius and founder of an entire generation and style of dance and music, really. I've been here for ... a little while.

My journey over was a difficult one. I was in a very drugged and difficult state when I left the Earth plane. I had been losing my grip on reality for quite some time. My lifestyle in itself was a very strange thing, now that I look back on it. I was raised and lived in a cage all my life. I really had no freedom as such; I found freedom within it. I got lost in the music and the dancing. I loved that. I loved the extreme focus my life had, but it did not allow me to balance myself. It did not allow me to have a healthy and happy family; it did not allow me to have healthy and happy friendships because of the contamination of fame and wealth and the observation of cameras wherever I went. It was quite difficult.

I have found friends here who have suffered the same fate, and we have discussed it. This is why I am participating in this book. I am not normally apt to do something like this, but since I have come over, since I have experienced life after death, I understand my life more. I understand what people wanted from me and what they were asking from me. Little did they know, they were taking from me some very important parts of my life that I needed to function properly. They took away my privacy; they took away my peace of mind. They took away my ability to be free, and it was these things that drove me, in the end, to seek relief from my own existence in drugs. It was this that caused me to attack my body.

In hindsight, I understand this now. I did not see it this way at the time; I did not see that I was attacking my body through the plastic surgery processes I was going through, but now, as I look back on my experience, I was trying to change myself. I was just trying to change myself. I thought that if I changed myself physically, I would change myself mentally and emotionally, and that, of course, is not the case. When you have a surgery with this in mind, you look at the physical results and see that there are some, but you did not get the effect inside that you wished to achieve. So then you choose another surgery, and you hope this one gets you closer to where you want to be. But you cannot see it clearly, for your vision is distorted and you do not see yourself clearly. I did not see myself clearly.

When I came over here, once I had woken up from the sleep in which I found myself ... it was not a tormented sleep. It was a heaviness, a druggedness. I had not been myself for some years without drugs in my system, so my clarity of thought was quite impaired and I needed some time, when I first came over, to learn to be in my own mind again. With the removal of the drugs, with the removal of the ego's layers of conditioning, I was able to clearly see my life. I was able to see clearly, and I was, I have to say, somewhat horrified by where I had ended up.

It is a humbling experience to look at a life you thought was very successful and see that there were many decisions you made that were less than ideal and that led you down a path of inebriation, paranoia, and in the end, disaster.

My best experience in coming over was this clarity of vision and love of self, which I never really experienced on the Earth plane. I experienced this complete understanding and acceptance of who I am. I experienced a complete clarity of vision, an understanding of all of my decisions, their confusion, and their intent. All of these things become clear to you [in the afterlife], and you look back with absolute forgiveness on yourself and with absolute forgiveness on all other beings, for you see them clearly too. You see that their intentions, even though they may have felt cruel from your own experience, were meant to be loving. You see that their own intentions, even though they felt manipulative, were an attempt to receive benefit somehow. This is what allows you to come to a place of complete peace.

It's hard for you to imagine this when you live in your mind with all of its twists and turns. On Earth, it is very difficult to imagine coming to this place of absolute peace, absolute joy, and absolute acceptance of all of the circumstances of your life, but that is why they call it heaven, I suppose. It is heaven to be free to think, to be free to create without manipulation, without anybody wanting you to do anything, without anyone adoring you. This is one of the most amazing things for me, as somebody who was never treated as an ordinary being by anyone — except perhaps my children. They were probably the only ones who treated me as an ordinary being, and for that I will always be grateful because it grounded me, in some sense, in the world.

Here I am just one of many. I am just one of many beings who experiences this other world, this after-death life. And so we work in music together. There are wonderful studios here where you can create amazing music, music that you can actually see dancing in the air in the form of light and other shapes. It is quite spectacular. It is quite overwhelming at times, the beauty of it. We spend our time here working on new compositions, working on new dances, working on new arrangements, and there are many beings who inspire those of you who are still in your bodies with these angelic songs.

It is quite fascinating for me as a musician, as a composer, and as a creator of these kinds of things to see how the information is transmitted down into the Earth sphere, for you do think, when you are a musician, that these ideas and these inspirations are your own. When you actually see the energetic structures through which they are transmitted, it is quite fascinating. You can inspire people on Earth if they are open and in a loving place, with no fears or judgments to cloud their receptors. You can influence them quite easily from this side with the creative processes.

Something else you can see from this side, which is quite distressing, are the lower realms where beings who are not at peace can influence other beings who are not at peace. When I look back on my life, there are times when I was in a bad place, a dark place, where I can look back and see that there were darker energies around me feeding off that, using that vibration as an access point into my life. It is quite important for you to know, as beings who are vibrational receivers, that this is what you really are. You do not feel that's what you are, but that is what has become clear to me since I have been on this side: that you are receivers. You are collectors of information, but you are also receivers of information, and this mixture creates the wonderful, unique being you are.

You are in your physical body experiencing certain things, and then there are these ideas that come to you from us, from beings in the nonphysical. These things mix together with your own thoughts and ideas, and you come up with new creations. You come up with new dances; you come up with new songs. You come up with new ideas.

That was what I was really excited to see, and now, on this side, as I work with music, I work with musicians and nonphysical beings who love music and are very joyful to be around. They take you to a level in which you have never participated before. They take you to expressions of creativity that, in the physical body, I had glimpses of. I understand now that they were trying to connect with me, but my mind was very polluted by negativity, insecurity, fear, and paranoia, and when you are on this side, each one of these levels of dysfunction prevents clarity of transmission from this side.

I was a big receiver in the sense that I was always dancing and I was always singing. Those were the times when I was open, and — fortunately for me — I had a great crowd of beings assisting me. This is why you saw such talent, such ease of performance for me — because that is when I was at home. I felt so good on stage because I was able to connect with this loving energy that permeated me from this side, and that is why I kept dancing. That is why I kept performing — because when I was not, I sunk back down into my mind that was contaminated with these misperceptions and I lost that wonderful feeling. But as soon as I got on a dance floor, as soon as I began to sing, I connected with them again. I did not realize, of course, that this is what I was doing. If I had known, I would never have stopped. If I had known, I would have taken this energy, this loving, spiritual, creative energy, into the rest of my day. But I did not understand how my mind worked.

This is why I want to participate in this sharing, in this book that you are reading right now, because you must understand that all of your negative thoughts are not who you are. They are based on things you have been told that are not true — perhaps by your parents, perhaps by your church, or perhaps by kids in your class. They are not true, but if you believe them, if you begin to judge yourself as others have spoken of you, you begin to lose this connection to joy, to creativity, and you begin to vibrate at a lower level. And then lower ideas and beings can come in contact with your mind, and it becomes a vicious circle.

This is very important, and this is why I am sharing this with you — because it would have saved my life, and I would have been able to continue on if I had wanted to. I would have been able to continue on. I would have lived a different life if I had known this information, so this is what I want you to know. I want you to monitor your thoughts. I want you to understand that your thoughts are vibrational. Just as the beings here have these high, high, loving, vibrational thoughts, many of you on Earth have low-vibrational thoughts, and this is what I suffered from. I suffered from some of these thoughts, and it disconnected me from the truth of who I am. It disconnects you from the truth of your true experience.

I was lucky. I had my creativity as a lifeline, and I would grasp it when I went too low, but many of you do not grasp a lifeline because you are not connected to your creative nature. This is what I wish for you to understand: Your creative nature is one of the most open and clear connections to Spirit, and if you can, begin to get into your creative vibration. If you can, begin to get into your creativity, no matter what it is. It doesn't matter what you do. It doesn't have to be music; it can be anything you love that brings something new into the experience. When you are in that mode, beings of a higher vibration are able to connect with you because creativity is what you call God. That is what it is: God is creative. God has created the realms that you see and that you don't see. God has created love; God *is* love. So when you are in a vibration of creation, you connect with that Source energy that wants you to thrive, that wants you to expand and evolve your consciousness. This is why it provided such a balm for me. This is why it provided such relief for me from the world.

I am happy here. I am a little ... bruised, still, when I focus my mind on my life, because I see that many of the stories that were told around me are not true. I see that many of the activities I participated in were confused attempts on my part to find peace, but I did it the wrong way. I did it through isolation and through focusing on money, material possessions, and the isolation that wealth can bring. It is not a fault, per se;

as I look back, I can see that I was doing all I knew to protect myself from the attack of the celebrity-manufacturing machine that is the twenty-first century, the twentieth century. I was doing all I knew how to do. I look back, and I have a few feelings of regret, but I must understand. I must forgive myself for the decisions I made based on a warped sense of self, the decisions that came from this intense focus I had on me my whole life.

I was not allowed to be a child in the sense that most children are allowed to be children, so I was trying to have that experience of innocence and joy in the extreme spending and recreation that I participated in, that I created for myself. The world of celebrity, money, and fear mixes up into a poisonous brew, and it is really a difficult thing to look on, for I only ever enjoyed creating and singing.

I didn't want the rest of that life. I didn't want the rest of it. It is fun in the beginning when you first become famous and people want you, but you realize that they don't want you for you; they want you for what they can get from you, and that is the hardest part. So you set up defenses, you set up perimeters of security, and you set up walls around yourself, yet you cannot survive that way. It is very difficult to live in celebrity. I enjoy the freedom I have here to just participate in creativity joyfully and happily with other beings, some of whom I've known on Earth, who are musical, who share this experience, who have shared some things in common with me on the physical plane. But we don't talk about that, really; we really immerse ourselves in what we are doing here. I only share myself with those beings of a higher vibration, and I look forward to inspiring some earthbound beings who are musicians and singers with the newfound joy of creation I am experiencing here.

My take on this whole thing is that you must understand that you are a vibrational being, that you are a receiver of information as well as a collector of information. If you understand that balance, then you can begin to incorporate spiritual inspiration with your own experience and come up with a healthy balance, a healthy view of what you are and what is going on in your experience. To be sucked into the world 100 percent is a very dangerous and frightening prospect.

We are all here — we who are in spirit, we who have affection for the world and the experiences there. We understand the suffering you go through when you do not understand the truth, and that is why I am participating in this book. I want to lend my name, a name that is very well known and around which people have a great curiosity. I want you to know that I am now experiencing life after death with other beings of like minds. I am happy in this creative process and recognize that it was the pure essence of what I was on Earth, but it was clouded. I want you to understand that all of my behaviors on Earth, no matter what you thought of them, were coming from the intent to give myself some peace and joy in my experience. As strange as they looked, they were an honest effort on my part to live life as well as I could. I ended up not doing a very good job, obviously, at the end, and that is why I am participating in this. That is why I offer my voice to this throng sharing our experiences here.

You are a vibrational being, and it is important that you understand this. Every thought you have, every food you ingest, and every idea that you entertain is of a certain vibration, and you want to make sure they are of *high* vibration. Make sure your thoughts are aligned with love, that your food and body are looked after. Do not ingest drugs as I did; it is a slippery slope and can get out of hand. And the ideas that you have — make sure you are only entertaining and focusing on the ones that bring you joy. If you have ideas and thoughts that are negative, turn your focus away from them, for they are not from here. They are from another place, a lower-vibrational realm where the light does not penetrate. If you focus too much on the darkness, if you focus too much on hatred, jealousy, or cruelty and let that become your life, you will not come to these higher realms. You will be forced to be with beings of like vibration, and you will be forced to return again and again to experience these darker aspects of yourself until you choose another way.

I am here with higher-vibration beings because I focused on love. I had very many twisted and incorrect ideas in my mind, however, and that took me down a path of less accomplishment and less strength, until I became so lost that I was called back home.

These stories I tell you about the lower vibrations are not punishments in any way; they are merely reflections of choices you make. So make sure your choices are for love. Make sure your choices are for creativity. Make sure your choices are for compassion and sharing and offering up your talents in a most honest way, and beware of the celebrity machine.

If you find you are creative, that you are beginning to be noticed by others, do what you can to *not* join in this celebrity machine. You may not make as much money down there, and you may not get the big roles and the big numbers that I got, but protect your life. Protect the ordinariness of yourself. There is nothing wrong with being a creative being with an ordinary life. Those dreams you have of extreme fame, extreme wealth, and extreme celebrity are just that — dreams — and they are dreams that have been fed to you by the machine that wants you as fodder.

That is my advice to you: Be creative, but do not be too ambitious. Be careful what you wish for, for the extreme fame that I received was not beneficial to my experience. It was not beneficial to my happiness. I am happy now; I am creative now. I am merely enjoying my experience after a long and tiring life. The time is faded now, though; I am in a timeless place. I do dip down once in a while to look at the world and see what is happening, to hear the stories that are still being told about me. I'm sure they will go on for quite some time, but I am creating a new life here, a new experience, and I am full of gratitude for the understanding that I have come to about what I did and what I didn't do, and for the gratitude of the peace, beauty, and unconditional acceptance and love that I find here.

My story from this side is not a juicy gossip column, as you perhaps were hoping for. I am merely telling you to watch your vibrations and watch your thoughts. Make sure you are aligned with the highest of beings, and you will do well. You will thrive and receive great inspiration from this side — and perhaps even from me.

CECIL B. DeMILLE

1981–1959

Cecil B. DeMille was an actor, director, and producer who became a giant of the twentieth-century film industry, known for epics like The Ten Commandments.

TINA'S COMMENTS

YESTERDAY I WAS FILLED WITH THE DESIRE TO PAINT. It is coming through to me, loud and clear, as I travel through this experience, that the gift of creativity is the most important. How sad it is that for so many, creativity is considered the footnote to life and not the focus.

I have created all my life to one degree or another, working as an artist for the past seventeen years or so, and I am convinced now — after hearing these tales of the importance of creativity — that this is part of the reason Ananda was able to come through. At times I was quite militant about my painting, refusing to do dishes or cook because I saw those things as blocks to my life's purpose. In hindsight, I wasn't too far off the mark, it seems. Ananda assured me this morning that all of this writing, designing, and channeling is also creative and I should not get hung up on the painting as a more valuable expression; it is not. All creativity, whatever its shape, is of great import in our connection to Source.

This morning's visitor was very grand in feel and had very intense facial expressions as he spoke. He had one of the more intense physical expressions of this montage of speakers. Once again, he is a being with whom I have no affiliation, but he has something he wishes to share with us all!

CECIL B. DEMILLE'S MESSAGE

WE ARE HERE! Yes we are, we are. We are very happy to be here. We have been here for quite a bit of time and are enjoying ourselves, we would say.

It is an interesting environment in which you find yourself after you have passed on. It's an interesting environment in which you express yourself after being in the physical body. It does fade very, very quickly once you get here, though. It is not something you really hang on to; it's not something that you really ... uh ... miss. You imagine, in this world in which you live, that this body you find yourself in that is so overwhelming when you are in it is going to be a loss. [*Chuckles.*] It is so not the case. The loss of the body is the biggest gift of the whole experience. It is not something you attach to at all; it's not something you miss at all. It is like you have taken off something tight — a wet suit that is sticky and confining — and you are released into a world of great beauty and freedom.

My name is Cecil B. De Mille. I am a director and filmmaker, and this is a wonderful opportunity to speak about the world in which I lived, in which I produced many movies, and in which I controlled many people's lives. This was something that was very necessary to my ego at the time — to feel powerful, to feel in control of things — and that was a wonderful experience for my ego. However, when I died, I just really had a different opinion of everything.

I looked back on some of the power I wielded, and I did not feel like I had done the very best that I could have done. But hindsight is always 20/20, isn't it? It is always much easier to look back on errors and understand them, but here you have the magnificence of the view of truth. You have the magnificent understanding of a complete vision of the world — all its meaning and all its requirements for learning and consciousness raising.

Of course, my first idea when I got here was that I would like to make a movie of it. Ha! I thought this would be a wonderful movie, but you cannot convey the comprehension level of the experience. You cannot convey the love level of the experience as you pass into this new realm. You could not convey this in any way. Really. People have no way of expanding their consciousness as they watch a movie, so that is a very difficult thing to do, really.

I have been enjoying it here, although I am coming to the end of my time as this consciousness that you would consider Cecil B. DeMille. I am shifting and changing now to prepare for a new incarnation. What happens is this consciousness, this focal point that you would call a personality, begins to integrate all of the information that the oversoul has collected over time through different incarnations that are past, present, and future — and all happening at the same time.

This is something that is very difficult for you to understand. The linear structure of your mind is not suited for this, and your linear structure of mind is there for a reason. It is there so you can experience physical sensations and creative experiences in a moment of time. You have to be able to focus to do this. This is very much like using a camera, for example: If you do not focus on anything, you cannot comprehend the scene. It is only in the structure — the background, the foreground, and the focal point — that you begin to see the structure of the scene and understand what is happening. This is like life. You must focus on what is happening in the moment or you will not understand it. The same thing happens within an individual's perceptual experience in a given moment, but it also is in the oversoul's experience of life that they ... they are not a "they." They are a higher consciousness aspect of yourself. You are an element of them as a flower is an element of a flower plant, as a leaf is an element of a tree. We are an element of the oversoul that collects information.

So now I am going to prepare to stop focusing in this consciousness of this incarnation that you are familiar with as a producer of movies. I am going to go into another life to experience some of the things I created in this past incarnation. There is some misunderstanding that needs to be corrected. I did wield a great deal of power, and at times I had the power to destroy beings — and did so without compunction. I would not return a call, or I would not give a part, or I would not condone somebody's contract, and I would ruin a life. And I would do it without care. I would do it for the betterment of my career, for the betterment of the current creative project I was involved in. This is one of the things I saw after I passed on — that I had, on occasion, actually ruined someone's life without thinking twice about it. I did something selfish and quite brutal, and people lost their livelihoods because of it — and often their families or their homes. I got to see this after I passed over. I got to see the consequences of my actions, and it was at times a little distressing initially because I did not realize what I had done. I did not mean to do that; however, I did do that. It was through my lack of compassion or lack of understanding of the total situation.

So, it is with this kind of lesson in mind that I will return to a position of power where I will attempt … for these memories do not go with you. The desire to change goes with you; the desire to learn a different lesson goes with you. But again, the same forces are nipping at your heels — the forces of the material world. It requires a decision of conscience to achieve these goals. As you go through many different experiences, many different incarnations, you are given a greater and greater impulse. And if you do not achieve it initially, you will come back again and see that you have not been able to transform yourself in the same way once again. You will be given the lesson again, and this time it will become louder and the impetus will become stronger, yet the barriers will also be there. It seems as if this is a cruel joke of the universe, but from conscious awareness — which is what you experience when you analyze these life incarnations — you see that it overcomes the barrier and focuses your attention on a particular goal that is the learning experience. If it comes too easily and flops into your lap like a dead fish, then you do not appreciate it; you do not comprehend it in a visceral and pointed way.

This is where determination and ambition kind of work in your favor, but you must understand that compassion and forgiveness must be part of your life experience. You do not have to be mean, you do not have to be insensitive or cruel, and you do not have to wield power with a heavy iron fist to achieve your goals. In fact, if you are nicer to people as you travel up your ladder to success … if that is what you choose to experience. It seems to be something that I enjoy doing — being successful in that worldly sense. There is no judgment on this side whether you are a farmer in the dirt or you are a queen. There is no judgment, no greater or lesser, in your experience on this side.

This is also something that is important for you to know: Just because I have a name you recognize does not mean I wield any more spiritual power than anybody else does. And because you do not have a name, perhaps, in your world, in this physical incarnation in which you find yourself, it does not mean you are of no consequence. We are of equal consequence. This is the message of the book, of course, and this was one of the reasons I was corralled into doing this. I say that word ... of course I am happy to do it, but I am being dramatic. I am being the star that I am! Of course, I am pulling your leg; I am joking, for I am not a star here. I am not the big controller here. I am the learner; I am the student; I am the understander; I am learning to understand. That is my take on this matter.

I was not particularly easy-going person, but that is not necessarily a detrimental experience for those beings around here, for they have to learn their own power. Sometimes this is a lesson of working with someone who wields a lot of power in the material world. You are forced to develop your own strength. And this is one of the other aspects of life in physical incarnation that is very interesting once you get back here: You realize that there were beings with whom you had conflict or with whom you had disputes or love relationships, and you realize that you had an agreement with all of these beings — that they would provide you with hurdles or helping hands throughout your journey. You realize that this was all orchestrated and played out like a wonderful symphony: Each being in your life played the part of a different note, a different musical instrument within the symphony. There are loud phases, there are quiet phases, there are solos, and there are duets in the symphony, and these all play a part in your life. As you pass over, you feel this wonderful comprehension of the complexity and organization that went into your experience.

There are times when you will see that you completely misunderstood the relationship that was presented to you. An opportunity that was presented to you slipped by because of your conditioning and your self-centered view of things, but that is not punished. It is merely offered up for repetition. It is merely offered up again in the new life's design so you can once again try to experience that.

I hope this has been helpful. I hope you see that you are, in your ordinariness, no less valuable than these famous names who show up in this book to share their stories. Your story will be as interesting and as valued by the consciousness that you are contributing to as mine or Marilyn Monroe's would be. You are given a design for your life that is driven by your intuition and your feeling/guidance system, and it will take you exactly where you need to go, so listen to how you feel. Listen to those little voices inside that suggest you go left or right or to phone somebody up. This is how the communications from the nonphysical are conducted — through the receiver that is your brain, your mental consciousness. Do not flounder around, listening to other peoples' opinions. Do not be cruel, and do not be so self-centered in your journey that you do not offer kindness and sympathy to others, but do not let them stop you on your journey, for they have their own and you have yours. It is important that you follow yours, for your lessons are yours to learn. If you are too distracted and you are put upon by too many people asking you to do things for them all the time — as many of you are — you will miss your purpose. You will your vision that you set for yourself as you arrived in this physical incarnation, and you will kick yourself a little bit at the end of your life, realizing that you made too many sandwiches and cups of tea for other people who didn't care whether or not you achieved your own ambition.

It is a balancing act, of course — like anything is. It is a balancing act of cooperation, of individual creative expression, and of this understanding that your guidance system — your emotions, your feelings, your dreams, and your ideas — comes from some nudging from the nonphysical. It's best to listen to them because if you do not listen to them and get caught up in the physical world, you will not manifest these great accomplishments that you are destined to.

You are not all going to be famous; that is not the point of this message. The point is you have a creative expression that you wish to pursue. You may be a fantastic gardener, a fantastic cook, or a fantastic mother, but each of these is going to be driven by your internal guidance system, which will give you the desire to do something, to experience something.

I am going to be manifested on the plane in the form of another being who is creative in a space of power, and I will have the opportunity, once again, to hone my skills, for if you do not master your particular incarnation's lessons, you will get another opportunity. It is not a punishment;

it is an opportunity for further growth and understanding, and you will mix it up again — coming back to give it another shot, so to speak.

Do not fear death. Do not fear this passing over. There is not one iota of it that is unpleasant; there is not one iota of it that is cruel, judgmental, or punishing in any way. That story is a lie; it is not the truth of this experience. It is a freeing, wonderful, educational, creative, and joyful expansion. That is it. That is all it is — a wonderful, wonderful experience.

That is all I wish to say. I am now going to go off and do what I do here, which is commune with other beings of creative mind, and I will return to Earth sometime soon to begin a new journey and a new life on Earth. Enjoy your life on Earth, for it is a wonderful gift. Do not waste it. Do not be cruel. Be creative and firmly placed on your path, knowing that you are motivated by divine desires. That is it. That is my message.

JONAS
SALK
1914–1995

Jonas Salk was an American physician and medical researcher who developed the first safe and effective vaccine for polio.

TINA'S AND ANANDA'S COMMENTS

HERE IS MY MORNING MESSAGE FROM ANANDA about the book and some of the feelings and things I am experiencing as I channel this material. This gives you an idea of the kinds of things Ananda says to me before each transmission — comments, advice, assistance, and explanations:

We are with you again, dear one. You are fresh and rested after a long night of dreaming and interacting with us. We are constantly working with you on the nonphysical side throughout your dream time, for you are free of your constraints. You are free of your small, conditioned mind; although, your small and conditioned mind expands as we push at the boundaries of its limitations.

This is what you were feeling yesterday; you were feeling a shift in consciousness as the magnitude of this project is coming into your awareness. You are bumping up against these ideas of potential criticism from the outside world, the feeling that you will be laughed at for producing this work, and the idea that it cannot be true, for there are too many famous people together in one room, so to speak. But you must understand that in the nonphysical world, these beings are not famous at all. They are ordinary beings, and it is no different than a room full of fifteen ordinary people sharing their ideas and experiences.

Fame is a product of your culture, a product of your misperceptions. These beings are no more exceptional than any of you. You all have the ability to shine; you all have the ability to be beautiful; you all have the ability to change the world. These are merely beings who did that, to one degree or another — better or worse than others. They had this experience, and they came into a culture that is obsessed with celebrity, and had this culture not existed, they would have been, perhaps, the most attractive people in their villages. They would have been the most talented artists in their villages. These kinds of things are how it would have been, but because of the machine of celebrity, because of this idea of marketing, these beings have become stars so big that you cannot imagine that they are ordinary human beings. But from a nonphysical point of view, they are all equal, as you are all equal.

This is part of the message, is it not? Not one of you is more valuable than the other. Not one of you is more important than the other. Not one of you is loved in the eyes of God more than the other. This is a strong and powerful message from this book, and do not worry; we will write a wonderful conclusion that sums it all up, that gives you all of the information you need to come to a true comprehension of that which we seek to achieve through this transmission.

We have another being here who wishes to communicate with you, who wishes to share his experience with you. We have indeed noticed this thing — that if the name is not spoken early on in your transmission your thinking mind begins to interfere. So we are asking each of the beings who come forth to speak their names quickly and succinctly in the first sentence or two so that you do not begin to wonder, to engage your mental processes, for this interferes with the channeling process. You must be out of the way. So this has been noticed, this has been spoken, and you will find that the next being is a very interesting one — one you wish to connect with and will be fascinated to hear from.

So relax. Sit back in your chair. Think of this as someone tell-ing you a story — nothing more, nothing less. It is not up to you to think about what it means, where it is going, or what the implica-tions are. Just sit back, relax, and allow the being to communicate. Listen to the story with rapt attention, with joy, and with immense curiosity. This is what we ask of all of our readers and listeners, so this is what we ask of you, dear one. You are the same. You are the channel, but you do not know this information, and you do not know these beings. They have stories to tell you, so relax, sink back, and trust in the process.

JONAS SALK'S MESSAGE

I AM A BEING WHO HAS BEEN HERE FOR A WHILE NOW. My name is Jonas Salk. I am a medical person, an inventor, and a developer of what you would consider one of the most transforming events on your planet — the idea of inoculation, the idea of vaccination. I developed many such products when I was alive, and I have come for a specific purpose.

I have come to talk to you about the process of vaccination and inoc-ulation as it happens on your planet at this time. There was an original design in this idea to assist beings from losing so many children, to assist beings in promoting health. There was a simple process involved of the understanding of the body's immune system. This is the project I worked on, the project I developed: the system that prevented so many young deaths, so many tragic occurrences that broke the hearts of many par-ents, that ruined and took away the lives of many children.

It was not necessary, we found out, for this to happen in such huge numbers, so we developed systems to prepare the body's immune system in advance of the attack of these viruses and germs that were causing such devastation in the population at the time. This work was very exciting. I was passionate about it. I had every ounce of my being invested in this interpretation of information. The ideas were coming fast and furious, and the inspiration was powerful indeed. I had no choice but to get up every morning in my life and continue the work, continue the development of these wonderful chemicals that changed the lives of many. I was very, very excited at this time in my life when these developments were happening.

I come to you now with a different story. I come to you now, watching what is happening to the youngsters of this planet, watching what is now being injected into their systems, and I speak up for a reason! I speak up to tell you to stop this insanity, to stop this big business that is perpetrated in the governments and schools and systems that permeate your culture. Your children are being poisoned. Your children are being killed. Your children are being injected with things that are not good for them.

The purpose of my work was to prevent the carnage that was happening through disease at that time, but what is happening now is that the big business of pharmaceuticals, the big, big business of the "health" industry … and I use that word "health" very loosely. It is not based on health at all; it is based on sickness. This is what is happening in your inoculation and vaccination systems: You are being duped by big business. You are being duped by people who are making millions, billions of dollars off your fear of losing your children, and it has gone too far.

It is time somebody who has some clout in this particular arena of business spoke up. I understand, of course, that most scientists won't listen to a book such as this, but we hope there will be somebody somewhere who has an open mind and an open heart and cares for the well-being of the youngsters of this planet.

Big business has taken over the idea of this inoculation and vaccination business, and they are instilling in you fears of plague and outbreaks of things that will not happen. You are injecting too many chemicals that are deadly and too powerful into small bodies that cannot handle it. You must understand: There is nothing wrong with inoculation against fatal diseases that will devastate populations over time, but there is no reason to inoculate children against diseases that are childhood experiences that develop your immune systems. This is what you must understand. The immune system is a system that works through challenge. It is like your body: If you sat in a bed all the time and did nothing, your muscles would not develop, and they would atrophy. You would be weak. You would be comfortable for a little while, but you would find that the system of your body needs stimulation. It needs growth; it needs challenge. Your immune system is exactly the same. Your immune system develops through challenge. It develops through encounters with these bacteria, with these germs, and with these viruses. It develops its strength through this very process.

What is happening is you are keeping your immune systems in bed, and you are poisoning your physical bodies with chemicals and cocktails of dangerous substances that wreak havoc within your bodies. And, indeed, you are seeing negative consequences. You see allergies, you see cancers, you see autism, and you see learning and mental/emotional disabilities that are caused by this massive influx of chemicals to the young bodies of your children.

It is time for parents to step in and say, "Enough!" Immunize them against these life-threatening diseases of smallpox, scarlet fever, diphtheria, and whooping cough. There are a few that are significant — there is no doubt about it — but they have almost been eradicated, so you do not need to fear a massive outbreak. If you all stopped immunizing today, nothing would happen for a long, long time, for the germs and viruses that cause these diseases have been eliminated to such a degree that it would take centuries for them to develop again into the strong waves of plague that they used to be.

You are indeed poisoning your young children. You are indeed harming them. For goodness' sake, if you have a baby in your belly, or if you have a baby in your arms, do not allow these massive quantities of chemicals to be repeatedly injected into their little bodies! You are being indoctrinated into a system of sickness manufacturing that is based on money, and there are no two ways about it. You are being indoctrinated into a system of "health" care, and again, I do not like this word "health," but it is the phrase you understand in your time and place. We will put it in quotation marks because it is not health; it is a lie. You are being indoctrinated into a system that wishes for you to be weak, that wishes for you to fail, that wishes for you to use its products and its ceremonies to keep yourself going. Their business is sickness, and their business is the manufacturing of sickness.

The individuals involved in these systems do not understand what they are doing, but the developers of these systems have a purpose and a goal, and that is only to make money. They do not care for the health and well-being of your beautiful little babies. They do not care for the health and well-being of these youngsters who need to grow and learn and have healthy bodies so that they can travel on their journeys. You must listen to your instincts, and your instincts will tell you — if you are quietly contemplating this prospect of injecting chemicals into your small baby's body, your heart will tell you not to do it. That is us on the nonphysical side telling you not to do it.

We are in force here, connecting with parents who are making this decision. We are trying to get you to stop. There is nothing wrong with saying, "I will take one small injection of one thing, and next year we will take one small injection of another thing." There is nothing they can do to force you. They can try to pressure you. We need to create a ground-swell of parents who refuse to inoculate their children with so many chemicals and so many antidisease medications that are not required. Your immune systems need to develop themselves, to be challenged. Your bodies need to be made strong by encounters with these diseases and viruses. There is a plan in this; there is a system in this. Your bodies are not weak. Your bodies are strong systems that will respond with their own natural mechanisms to foreign invaders.

As a scientist, as a developer of this system of transformation of the physical body, I say to you: Pay attention to this. Pay attention to me. I know of which I speak, and I ask you from the nonphysical to stop this fearful and over-the-top reaction to disease. What I am saying is that my life's work is now being contaminated. What I am saying from the nonphysical side is that my life's work has been turned into a murderer, a crippler, a damager of small children, and I will not stand behind it. I will not stand behind it from this side of the after-death experience.

I am working with scientists, people, and activists now who are inspired to stand up against this system. It is my voice they hear, for I am highly motivated to change this system that I instigated, if you will. I was in the beginning phases of it, but I no longer support it. I no longer throw my energy behind it, and I wish for you to hear these words.

Step away from these intense vaccinations that you are asked to give your children, and tell your doctors that you will not put that many chemicals in your new babies' bodies, for you love these beings and trust in the natural systems of the body. You will put one or two in occasion-ally, but they need to stop asking you to do so many, for you will not comply — for you love your children. You trust your children's physical strength and health, and you will not run in fear from these "boogey men" of diseases that no longer exist on your plane. You are creating a whole new world of problems, and the systematic damage that these chemicals cause to your babies' brains, to their physical structure, will be a curse that they live with their entire lives, and I will not support it. And I ask you not to support it.

This may seem a strange chapter in this book, for we have had these wonderful treatises and expositions on spiritual life, but you must understand that when your life's work is bastardized and changed into a murderous system, you cannot stand quietly on the sidelines any longer. This is the situation I find myself in. This is the situation that I am moved to speak to through this wonderful opportunity that this channel offers us — to speak our greatest truth, our most important message to the world.

That is my message: Stop vaccinating your children with poisons. Stop being motivated by fear. Trust in the health and strength of your bodies' magnificent systems of repair and defense, and all will be well. You will have children who are intelligent, strong, and whose systems work perfectly. These chemicals are detrimental and dangerous, and they are being sold to you by people who are making a lot of money. That is my message. That is my story, and I thank you so much for allowing me to share it in this format, for allowing me to share it in this way.

QUEEN
MOTHER
ELIZABETH

1900–2002

Queen Elizabeth was the queen consort of King George VI until his death in 1952. She is best known for her moral support to the British people during WWII and her longevity.

TINA'S COMMENTS

I AM NOW IN THE PROCESS OF EDITING and reworking this material for the book, and I have just listened to the following treatise by the Queen Mother. What eloquence and what a seamless expression of ideas and concepts you will find in this chapter! I am repeatedly blown away by the streams of consciousness that come through in this book, and I am also humbly amazed that they are coming through me in this way. What a gift, what an experience I am having! So many times I can see that people think the spiritual life is boring or uneventful, that in turning off their televisions they will be losing out somehow. Trust me — "boring" and "uneventful" are not words I use to describe my life.

QUEEN MOTHER ELIZABETH'S MESSAGE

I AM HERE. Yes, I am here. It is a great opportunity to be here and share this creative process that you are involved in. It is so wonderful to enjoy this venue, and I am happy to contribute my knowledge and experience to this process. It is unusual, very unusual indeed, this process of communication, this process of once again sharing of our nonphysical selves with the physical world that we participated in so fully and with such confusion at times.

It was a great shift in consciousness for me when I passed over. I am the Queen Mother; I am the wife of the king that was. But in my own right, I had a very interesting life, and I had a very … it was not confusing as such at the time; it was much more confusing after I passed over. I have been here a while, it is true, but I still, at times, do not understand the very different nature of the physical world from the nonphysical world. In a way, it was a journey of awakening when I came over on this side, and there were so many aspects of my life that were not what I thought they had been.

The extreme fame and restrictions of the monarchy are not easy to come to terms with once you have passed over. You see, so many of the protocols and rituals and restrictions that affected my life, that affected me as I journeyed through this experience, were pointless, pointless events. They hold no purpose whatsoever in the grand scheme of things, and it is very interesting to have lived a life of meaningless events, of these protocols, these façades, that were so very elaborate and so very limiting for the humans involved — not only for myself and my family, who I look down on now.

There are changes coming. There have been some changes, of course, from the younger people who tried to shake it up a little bit, but it is a very old and entrenched belief system. I fully support any changes that need to … that *are* made, for as a spiritual experience, the fame and the royalty — and the notoriety, if you will, of the inability to have an ordinary life — restricts rather than enhances one's spiritual growth. There is a tremendous amount of power, of course, but it is so circumscribed by these rituals that you lose sight of what you are capable of achieving in your life.

My personal experience of looking back on my life was one of great compassion, really — that is the word I would use. I can see that many of the shortcomings I may have had — and there were some, of course — were mostly influenced by the circumstances into which I was born. And from this point of view, I see that I was born into it for a purpose.

I was born into it to understand the rigors of public life and obligation of circumstances that do not really feel like your own doing. As I passed through this interpretive journey, through my life, it became clear to me that there were things that did not benefit me in a way. The restrictions on choice are a difficult cross to bear; there is no doubt about it. The restriction of choice is one of the things that truly go against what we are.

You would think that in a family such as the one in which I was incarnated there would be much choice, but the truth of the matter is there was not much choice. There were so many rules, so many people around all the time, and so many public obligations that "freedom" is not a word that I would have used at all to describe my incarnation.

When I arrived here, it was with great pleasure that I encountered absolute freedom, for here you can do that which you choose to do whenever you choose to do it. There are no restrictions. I participated with such joy in these newfound freedoms, for that was what I shed when I passed over — the cloud, the cloak of oppressive ritual.

This is my story that I wish to tell you: that habitual living, dictated to you by other beings, is not in your spiritual interest. It does not serve you to do the same thing all the time because it is comfortable — a ritual, a habit that does not bring you what you want. It is very important for you to look objectively at your life and see if the habits you have serve you. It may seem strange for someone of royal blood to be telling you this mundane information; however, this is the other side of the coin that we face when we die: There is no such thing as royalty in spiritual terms; it is merely a group of beings who express specific circumstances to achieve certain spiritual and learning goals.

So here I am, somebody you would consider royalty, somebody you would consider above your station, but that is not the case at all. I am merely your equal. I am merely another being who had an experience and wishes to share her understanding of it.

That is the thought I would like you to keep in mind as you listen to this advice from a royal being: I am not royal at all; in fact, I am as you are: a sacred being. We are all sacred beings on a journey to awakening, collecting information, creating, and experiencing so that we may understand the complexities of ourselves more and so that we may understand the complexities of this universe. Although at times it appears to have many, many faces, the truth of the matter is quite simple:

freedom, creativity, and love. Those are the words I would use to show you what you should focus on — not ritual, habit, judgment, and fear, which is what so many of you are immersed in in this world these days.

Focus on love, creativity, and facing your own self-expression. Your self-expression is the most wonderful of joys, and it is through that form that I play with the reality in which I live. But self-expression in my life was not something that I was very privy to. I was able to paint or do those sorts of things, but the family obligations with which I was faced were so overwhelming, my conditioning to behave in a particular way was so strong, that I could not really express myself in any way that was meaningful.

That is one of the things I would like to say to you: Do not waste your life with bad habits and social constraints, with those thoughts and beliefs of others that keep you in your own little prison, your own little palace. The walls and the guards are your ideas about other people's opinions. The walls and the guards are your fears about stepping out of your conditioned mind into your full self. The walls and the guards are your habits, your bad habits that rule your body and your mind, preventing you from stepping out into new expressions of creativity and adventure. These walls and guards are not going to serve you. You will get to the end of your life, and when you pass over, you will get an opportunity to see what you have done with yourself, with your own experience, and you will see that there were many, many wasted hours and wasted years in mindless, unconscious behavior that did not take you along the path you had designated for yourself.

Some of these social pressures that come upon you seem to be other people's doing, but the fact is these are your own creation from your own experience and your own vibration. It is your job — although that is not quite the correct word … it is your purpose to overcome, to raise up your own vibration, to step into new arenas, and to come to new understandings. So when you find yourself trapped in a life you do not enjoy, which many of you have, we understand that. What you must understand is that you are a sacred individual, a free being, and nothing you do is required by what you would call this God.

There is no God being; there is only a loving energy that pervades all things, and it wants you to be in its vibration. It wants you to be able to accept this love, this wonderful abundance, freedom, and joy. But if you are trapped in a world that is uncomfortable, that is not pleasant, that does not reflect this higher vibration, then you must find a way to raise yourself up out of this situation, for it is through your own decisions that you are there. Are you drinking too much alcohol? Are you eating terrible foods? Are you judging your fellows on this journey? Do you hate other beings? Do you hate yourself? Are you consuming inappropriate materials, such as pornography or cheap and dirty gossip? These are the kinds of things that lower your vibration and keep you from achieving these wonderful aspirations you have set for yourself.

Some circumstances will be predetermined in the spiritual world, such as my birth into a royal family. That was not my conscious choice as a human. Of course, that was decided before I was born, and yet it was the lesson I was to learn. How much of an individual could I be? I came to learn the power of peer pressure. I came to learn the importance of freedom. These were the lessons I was meant to learn in this incarnation as a royal prisoner, let us say, but you have your own assignments.

So perhaps you are in an abusive marriage. Perhaps you are in a job that you hate. Perhaps you live in a way, in a place, that does not please you. You have been given these experiences to prove to yourself that you can overcome them. It is in overcoming them that you will achieve your true understanding of your glorious and powerful nature. That is what I advise.

If you look at your life and do not like what you see, begin now to step up to the plate. Begin to change yourself. Begin to focus on the most important area you would like to change. Is it your physical health? Is it your love relationship? Is it your work? It matters not. Whatever area causes you the most negativity is the one we suggest you begin to look at it and tackle. Begin to see what is being asked of you to overcome it, for that is the lesson. It is not to be punished by a God who does not love you; that is not the case. The circumstances do not arise as a testament to your unlovability. They arise as a testament to your strength and power in your potential ability to overcome them. So look around at your life. Look at the things you see. Look at the beings and the circumstances you are faced with every day, and ask yourself: What is it that you can do today to begin to change it? Do not come at it with a sense of hatred or impatience, but initially observe it and take it into your heart, knowing that its purpose to show you something about yourself that you have assigned to yourself in this physical incarnation, something you wish to overcome.

This is my advice as somebody who has spent her last incarnation constrained by ritual, by peer pressure, and by the obligations of a particular office. I felt this was where I did not shine, let us say. I did not reach my desired potential. I allowed others' wishes to overrule my own desires, and you cannot imagine more difficult circumstances to overcome. It was not that I failed completely, but I came to a true understanding of the importance of freedom and self-expression, and that was really why I was born into that particular incarnation — to come to this conclusion. So it was a success, as you can hear.

If you comprehend the answer to the question you asked before you were born, then your life is a success. From your point of view, it seems that that was a small understanding for such a large and imposing life, but the large and imposing life of fame is not what you imagine it to be. Many of our experiences are quite painful in that world. Many of our experiences are not what we seem to wish to experience, so it can be quite a struggle. Yet you look at the jewels and the clothes and the travel and those kinds of things, and you imagine that that life is so special, that it is so much more than yours. Let me assure you that it is not. It is of equal value to the mind of God, to the mind of the overall consciousness that expresses itself through us and through this physical experience you call your life.

That is my message: Do not give away your freedoms. Do not allow others to take your freedom. Insist on being free to make your own decisions, and if your family and your friends do not agree with you, then it is time to begin to introduce them to this idea of your free self, this self you have that has the right, the ability, and the need to express whatever inner being it wishes to express into this outer world. It is time that others understood you are able to be who you wish to be, that you are able to do what you wish to do, and that, really, it is none of their business.

Do not cow-tow to other beings in your life who wish to bully you, who wish to control you, who wish to take away your most basic of spiritual essences — which is the freedom of self-expression. This is our message to you. Express yourself in all your fullness with love and kindness to other beings. You do not need to attack them. If you do not attack back, the fight will go out of them, and if you merely seek your freedom quietly, initially, from the internal processes of your mind — focusing on that which you choose to focus on, reading about that which you choose to read about, studying that which you choose to study — you will find that your life will begin to change from the inside out. Then there will be inspired action as you begin to know yourself more, and you will begin to understand this process more. In reading books like this, you will come to a great understanding of what is important in spiritual terms, and it will be those focuses that will assist you in getting where you wish to go on this journey — to a full understanding of who you are and why you came, a full understanding of the magnificence of your spiritual expression in this physical world you call your life.

I will leave it there for now. I thank you for your time. I thank you for the interest you have shown in reading my small contribution to this book. It is not as magnificent on the outside as my life was, as my life appeared to be, but that is also part of the message: Your life does not have to be magnificent on the outside to be truly magnificent from the place of your own experience of it, for magnificence is in the appreciation of your life. Magnificence is in the love of those beings around you, and the magnificence of your spiritual expression as a physical being is in your freedom to be who you choose, your freedom to be what you choose. That is my message. That is what I wish to say.

GEORGE
BERNARD
SHAW
1856–1950

Irish playwright George Bernard Shaw wrote more than sixty plays during his lifetime and was awarded both the Nobel Prize in Literature and an Academy Award for his work.

TINA'S COMMENTS

I BEGAN TO HAVE THE URGE TO WRITE a spiritual book about five years ago, when I lived on a remote ranch as a caretaker. So I began the process, developing a plot and characters for what I called a "spiritual romance." During my youth, I had used romance novels to escape a world I did not really fit into or understand, and I truly wanted to write something that contained the spiritual principles that were helping me so much — disguised in an easily digestible package. Little did I know that my heart's desire would come true. It was not exactly as I had envisioned, but bigger and better than I could ever have imagined.

So it was with some interest that I read the following monologue, describing the importance of journaling and long-hand writing. That year I lived on the ranch, I filled dozens of journals with all kinds of musings, questions, and ideas, but I had no idea it was such a direct and influential way to connect with Spirit.

GEORGE BERNARD SHAW'S MESSAGE

I AM HERE. I am George Bernard Shaw, the writer and producer of many such things as plays, books, novels, essays — these kinds of things. I was known in my life as a famous author and have contributed much to the writing landscape you have experienced over the past hundred years or so. My plays are famous, my books are well known, and my image is easily called to mind by those beings in this world, although it is fading now as the modern era gallops along and the new technologies take over.

I would like to speak to this subject of handwriting. This is a subject that is very interesting as you go through your modernization process, your technological developments, and this audio-visual culture in which you find yourselves. As a writer, as a being who has participated in this process from both the physical side and the nonphysical side, it is very important for you to know that there is a connection that can be made through the mind, through the body, and through the physical apparatus of the writer who is writing long-hand with a pen, pencil, or such thing, which is not so easily made in the technological realms. There is something about the process of focusing the mind and the body at the same time that brings a very pointed experience, that brings a very decisive and focused attention to a particular subject. It allows the mind to clarify, categorize, organize, and integrate it in a way that does not happen in other processes. That is what I would like to discuss.

This may seem like some archaic old fellow promoting things that are out of fashion, but that is not the case. This is coming from a person who is in the nonphysical, who is experiencing this process in many different forms. Of course, now I am writing in my own way, in this astral form, and the process is much the same. The ideas arise in my mind, in my consciousness, and I execute them through my astral body, but we are also involved in communicating information to other beings, so this is different from the channel's experience.

As I am speaking, she is wondering how she can be such a clear channel for information. Well, she has done much work in areas of forgiveness and mental clarification that ordinary people generally are not involved in. We do hope that some of the materials that are being written here will assist in this process of clarification and understanding the importance of it. For those of you who are what you would consider ordinary beings, who are not channels of any kind or sort that you know of, long-hand writing is one of the ways we are able to influence you quite significantly. This is why I would like to speak to this subject, as there are fewer and fewer of you participating in this particular form of self-expression and self-analysis. You text, you type, you speak into computers, you make videos, and you do many things. These are all wonderful forms of communication that have their places, but from a spiritual point of view, sitting down, holding a pen or pencil, and quietly contemplating a subject — thinking about it, perusing it, investigating it in your mind —is the easiest form of expression through which we can assist you.

If you are struggling with a question, if you are struggling with a form of conflict in your life, or if you have an issue that is unresolved and you wish to resolve it, we suggest you begin to write down the possible solutions. This is one of the ways, as I said, that we can communicate with you in your modern world. Many beings over the years have been inspired in this way, of course. Many of your great novels — many of my writings — were inspired through connection to spiritual guides and muses, I would say, and I have come to understand this. At the time of my writings, I did not particularly understand this process, although I knew I was infused on many occasions with complete ideas that I merely transcribed into stories, essays, poetry, and other technical writing that I participated in.

I thought the ideas were coming from me, but of course, now that I have passed over, I am very well aware of the beings who participated in my creative process with me, who offered me assistance through the inspiration that came as I was writing. This is an important thing for you to understand as an ordinary being who has picked up this book, perhaps, because of the celebrities' names in it — because of the famous people you recognize. You are curious about what they have to say after their life experience. I may not be an important one of that group, but I am a writer, and as a writer and a person in the nonphysical, I see that this is the easiest format for spiritual beings who wish to connect with you to do so.

This is my contribution to the dialogue. It is not revolutionary; it is not an epiphany of any great import. However, if you could understand the tremendous potentials, if you could understand the purpose of your life, if you could understand that there is much rich information coming to you all the time, wishing to come to you all the time … But in your modern world, you are becoming more and more separated from the processes that facilitate this. As your minds are busied with these never-ending streams of information, with these never-ending devices that are always at your fingertips, taking your attention, taking your focus, you are losing connection to your spiritual guides. You are losing connection to your spiritual source of information and assistance.

Your lives will become more fractured. Your lives will become less cohesive, and they will become more annoying. They will become more agitated. So we recommend, as part of your spiritual practice, the daily and regular writing down of information for the purposes of spiritual connection.

We do not wish for you to think we are going to possess you in any way. There are fears in most of your Western minds around this subject. This is why we share this information in this strange and unusual way — because we wish for you to come out of this dark age of spiritual terror that has been perpetrated for many centuries on your world. It is ridiculous to be indulging in these ideas of possession and evil spirits lurking, waiting to get hold of you. We wish for you to understand that there are a plethora of high-vibration beings, beings who have had wonderful experiences and wish to share them, who have had transcendental lives of high spiritual vibration, who have great truths to share with you. They have knowledge of your purpose and your approaching life experiences, and they can assist you in clarifying your purpose and your creative connection to spiritual beings.

We know that many of you who have picked up this book are curious about the spiritual life, curious how it impacts this physical life you live. Well, let us tell you: From this side, we are often shocked when we first come back from our physical experience in the human body at how many opportunities we missed because we were misunderstanding, fearful, or ignorant of the processes of spiritual communication. The sheer number of beings who wish to connect, the sheer amount of information that is waiting to trickle down into your minds in the physical experience, if … these barriers to the fears around spiritual connection interfere with this communication.

If you want a simpler and more easily understood life, if you wish to find your life's purpose, if you wish to be included in the nonphysical dialogue, being given information that is very pertinent to your own spiritual development, your own physical health, and your own purpose on this plane, then begin to write. Begin to journal. But also begin to sit there, waiting for inspiration. Spend some days with a pen in your hand and an empty page in front of you. Ask for a subject about which you can write, and ideas will begin to flow. Do not be fearful. Do not think that something untoward will happen, but do be aware that your vibration should be in a place of high, happy, peaceful, and joyful curiosity. It should not be in a desperate, dark, and depressed place, for that is a vibration that you do not wish to continue. That is not a vibration with which you wish to connect further.

You must understand it is not of some evil vs. divine, demon against angel idea. It is merely a vibrational transmission. Make sure that you are on the correct vibrational transmission station, and you will receive the kind of information you wish to receive. If you have a problem, do not come at the pen with this problem firmly placed in your mind. Think about the problem, ask a question before you even come to the paper, and when you are sufficiently satisfied that the question has been posed, then we would like you to contemplate for a few minutes. Peacefully get yourself in a happy mood. Release the problem to the universe, to the higher realms of understanding, and come to your journal. Come to your creative writing process in a peaceful and calm mindset that will allow us to flow our energies into you.

This is a wonderfully exciting process to be involved in, and we hope that those of you who have picked up this text, who have picked up this book because of curiosity about celebrities, will be willing to venture into this little experiment, for your lives are becoming too disconnected from this process. Many of us reached our greatest creative expression through this process of sitting and writing, of composing music or art of some kind, yet you are losing this inspirational connection, this inspirational form of self-expression, expression from spiritual. We are here to remind you to take time each day to do this. Take time each day to sit with a pen and paper, calm your mind, and ask for the nonphysical to communicate with you in a loving and elevated way. You will be very surprised by the results. You have not been taught to do this; you have not been taught that there is this connection. Or for many of you, if you *have* been taught that there is this connection, you have been taught to fear it.

It is time for a new revolution in consciousness. It is time for a new expression of your inner being, and this is what we hope this book will help precipitate: a removal of fear from this connection, a deeper understanding of what we are up to on this nonphysical side, and a willingness to participate in a dialogue with those beings who appreciate you, who love you, and who wish to assist you on your journey. That is all I wish to say — short and sweet and to the point, as I always was in life. I hope you enjoyed this small contribution to this wonderful patchwork of spiritual information that will assist you greatly in understanding your own self-expression and your own connection to spirit.

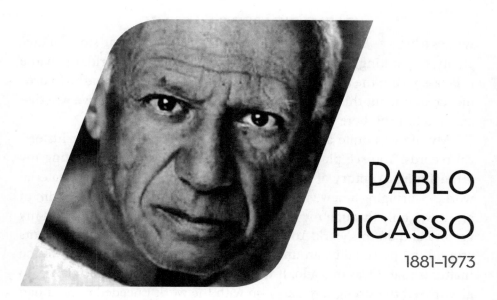

PABLO
PICASSO
1881–1973

*Spanish expatriate Pablo Picasso was one of the greatest and most
influential artists of the twentieth century, as well as the cocreator
of Cubism.*

TINA'S COMMENTS

I AM AN ARTIST, so it was with great interest that I finally found one
on this long list of people wishing to tell us about their life lessons. I
have always drawn, painted, or designed for my living, and I have often
wondered how people managed without art in their lives. For me, art is
a lifeline that keeps me sane in what I feel is an insane world, and I often
talk to people about how to become more creative, how to carve time out
of their busy days to tap into this wonderful and healing activity — often
attempting to convince them that art was more important than dishes or
vacuuming. The desire to create in me is stronger than almost anything
else, so it isn't really a struggle for me at all, and I have certainly come to
appreciate the freedom we now have to use color and pigment in any way
we choose. Apparently, I have Picasso to thank for that!

PABLO PICASSO'S MESSAGE

WE ARE HERE. Yes, we are here. We are here to share our story of creativity, of painting, of joyful, exuberant creation in this world. My name is Picasso. I am the artist of such renown, such arrogance, and such prolific creation, but this is not the story of my life — although we will discuss it a little bit here.

My life was quite an exciting one, as you know from your historical records. You see pictures of me; you see images of me creating my art, defining a century of modern art. That was my place in the material world — bringing a new vision to the creative expression in the realm of art. It was only through my abrasive qualities that I was able to stand my ground and do this work. You must see this. There are many judgments around my personality, around the way I behaved, but the truth of the matter is that it was bravado. It was a show to give myself confidence, to give myself the strength to carry on with the work I needed to do. I had this idea of how things could look. Obviously I was a skilled artist; I was able to follow convention, but I did not wish to. I wished to shake up the cage. I wished to rattle it and to create a new vision of the world, and I did.

That was my gift in my life — to free up the artistic realm for other beings, to allow them to express whatever it was that they wished to express from inside of themselves, without the rules and boundaries of ridiculous art conventions. As you can see, I was ridiculed. I was laughed at, yet my works became the most valuable. This is very important: Artists listening to this material, do not fall into the box of convention, because you do not honor the creative force that flows through you. The creative force that flows through you is the divine mind of God expressing itself, so do not let the small parameters of the human mind restrict you in your creativity. Do whatever it is that comes through, for art now is an open field, thanks to those beings like myself who crashed down the barriers, who crashed down the walls to this expression of self through this particular form.

I am now working on projects in the nonphysical, and this is strange to you. You may think that we do not continue our work as creative beings after we pass on — that we sit on clouds playing harps or some such thing. That is not the case. We are deeply immersed in creativity. We are able to create here. We are able to paint, to express ourselves in a very similar form, and the level of expression, the level of experience that we have here, is not so different — other than that manifestations appear very, very quickly, as in instantaneously, and you are able to change your environment very, very quickly. It is quite a surprise when you arrive here, where your thoughts are manifested and beings show up as soon as you think of them. Your feelings of smallness or negativity completely disappear once you arrive here. It is like a shell that is cracked off a baby bird; you feel like flapping your wings and flying, for you are not encased in the conditioned, habitual mind anymore.

When I came here, I realized I had been very cruel to some people in my life. I was very much of what you call an egomaniac. I controlled women, in particular, although I had been quite abrasive to many people I met. I was arrogant, and I was self-centered. The façade I developed to protect myself from the criticism of the artistic community had turned into a spiky, vicious outside that hurt beings who did not deserve any kind of attack on my part. This is what I saw after I died: that I had created a persona I ended up believing in. I ended up being cruel to people I should have loved. I ended up being disrespectful to beings who deserved respect, if for no other fact than that they are these wonderful spiritual beings experiencing their own expression.

As you come over to this side, you see that everyone is valuable. Everybody is of equal import in the collection and experience of creative force that is God expressing itself through the physical body of all the humans on the planet. There is not one — not one small child, not one old person, not one untalented factory worker — who is not as valuable as another. You even hear my judgments in what I say in that sentence. But the truth of the matter is you are given these different lifetimes to experience different experiences, and the experience you have of a famous personage is very different from the experience you have as a street cleaner. You must experience the dichotomy of these two things to understand what it is to be a human being through this deep comprehension of the equality of all.

This is a very interesting aspect of the fame experience, as this is part and parcel of this project's title. Being famous does not immunize you from anything. You are, if anything, faced with more difficult circumstances. You are faced with not only your private life, but your public life. For those of you who are not famous, do not dismiss your lives as unimportant because you are not famous. Be grateful that you have only one life to deal with. It is much easier to deal with one life than to deal with two that overlap and bump into each other and often are at odds. It is very difficult to have healthy relationships when you are famous. You have many people clamoring for your time, your body, your attention, and it is impossible, almost, to have a healthy, happy home life.

That was what I saw in my experience. I could have balanced my home life much more. I was so caught up in the fame machine, I was so caught up in being this famous artist, that I neglected other aspects of myself, and I spent a lot of time in the limelight lapping up the attention. In hindsight, I do have a few regrets in terms of my cruelty to people, but I have to say I did enjoy this lifetime of creation. I enjoyed this lifetime of celebrity, yet there was an aspect of myself that was not as loving or as kind as it could have been.

I suppose that is my message: Do not conform to society's expectations of your creativity. If you wish to paint your kitchen pink because it feels like you should do that, that is what you should do. You do not know where these creative forms will take you or how you will begin to express yourself. It is only in opening up the doors completely that you begin to allow the flow of information from the nonphysical.

There are many of us up here assisting beings who are creative in their expression, and if you seek divine intervention in paintings or sculptures you are creating, do not put up any barriers, for we cannot penetrate through them. Once you are open, once you ask for divine assistance from a place of high vibration, from a place of inspiration rather than depression … Do not contact us if you are depressed, for we cannot get to you. You are immersed in your own thoughts, and it is like armor: You cannot receive us. So clear the armor, get yourself upright, and get yourself happy. Do what you must to feel better. Begin to create, and we will be able to connect with you from this state. Open your mind, open your expression, and do not worry what people will think about it, for if you do, you will create within the box of convention, and that will not bring you anything. You will also put restrictions on those creative ideas that can come from the nonphysical, for we are here speaking to you, wanting to participate in your creativity through the idea of inspiration.

We do not force our ideas on you in any way, shape, or form, but we do inspire through image. We do inspire through feeling. We do bring our enthusiasm for creating into your world, and you will feel a great positive rush of energy, and that is us creating with you and excited.

The other message I have, of course, is to use your celebrity wisely. Use it for loving purposes. Use it for the enrichment and enlivenment of the planet. Do not use it for self-gratification, and do not use it for self-centered activities. Share your wealth, share your knowledge, and share your fame in positive ways so that you can influence those beings who need your assistance, those beings who could use your help. There is much power in celebrity, and there are many ways in which you can use it. There are many ways in which you can use the financial rewards of this particular form of expression — the famous artist.

If you are an artist and you wish to be famous, get yourself in a high-vibration state where we can connect with you, and we will join in with you, doing work that will inspire other beings when they see it, for it will be enlivened with divine creative expression. There will be many beings — not just myself — participating in this journey. We will, at times, show up as a group, conferencing with each other and discussing what will make a painting better or what we can do to assist you. Do not feel that you are alone when you are creating, for you are not. Be in a high spiritual place, a high-vibration place, free of intoxication and free of negative thoughts, and you will open a channel to the nonphysical where we can assist you, where we can help with that.

Creativity is a wonderful connection to Spirit, and it is one of the ways of initially opening up the channels between yourself and the nonphysical. It is a wonderful way for divine love and divine inspiration to flow into your world, into your mind, and into your body. You will feel the upliftment of it; you will feel the excitement of it.

As this being you call Picasso, I am changing my ways. I am becoming more loving; more kind; and more sharing of myself, my work, and my heart. This is my message: I am now being as kind as I should have perhaps been in my life, and I have learned that lesson from my life. This is what you must remember when you look around at beings who are being less than kind or less than perfect; you will know from my advice that their lifetimes will give them the illustration of what not to do and what not to be, and they will see when they look back over that experience that they have learned a lesson. They are indeed learning a lesson, even though they may look as though they are cruel and successful, even though they may look like they are inconsiderate and self-centered. They will have the experience, when they look back on their life, of seeing themselves in a different light and seeing the error of their ways. This is how you learn!

So do not judge your fellow travelers. Do not judge those whom you see misusing their power, but merely choose to use your own, when you receive it, in a way that is beneficial to humanity and to the creative and self-expressive life you have. You have it to live it. You have it to express it. Do not hide it. Do not be afraid to express it. Do not be shy. Do not let fear prevent you from creating that which is inside you, that which wishes to flow through you. That is my message: Be brave, be kind, and understand that those of us who broke the rules needed to be a little tougher to do that. Forgive us our harsh ways, for we believed our own marketing and believed our own stories. Forgive us for that, for we did not know what we were doing, really. We were merely unconscious beings believing in the roles we had decided we would play, and now we look back and see the truth of the matter — that we could have been better. But we did the best we could, and you will do the best you can.

Take the information from this book and employ it in your lives. Know that if you are powerful, then you need to use your power wisely or you will come back in a lifetime to experience that which you inflicted on others. This is not done as a punishment but so that you understand what it is like and truly learn not to do it again. That is my advice, for I will indeed be sent back at some point — when I am ready — and I will be given the opportunity to experience the treatment I inflicted on others. This will be a challenge, no doubt, but I understand the grand design behind all this, and I understand the purpose now. But your opportunity here, in reading this book, is to understand the design and the grand purpose before the end of your lives so that you can focus in a kind, loving, creative, magnificent, and self-expressive way. That is my message. Go forth and do that kindly. Go forth and do that exuberantly. Go forth and do that with great courage and great enthusiasm!

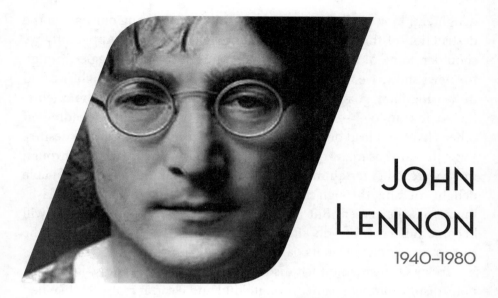

JOHN
LENNON
1940–1980

*Famed singer-songwriter John Lennon founded the Beatles, a band
that impacted the popular music scene like no other before or since.*

TINA'S COMMENTS

THIS MORNING I WAS TOLD that we have only one more person after
today's communication. So this book is coming to an end, and I have to
say, what a challenge this has been for me! I had a lot of resistance at first,
sometimes blocking the transmission with my own thoughts, trying to
figure it all out. Toward the middle of it all, I was more enthusiastic, waking each morning to see who would speak and what they had to say. And
now? Now I'm getting nervous again. Who will the last person be, and
what will the message contain?

My dear teachers Ananda told me this morning to expect derision
and ridicule — that this would be guaranteed, given the nature of our
society. That doesn't really make me feel any better, but I suppose this is
what I have agreed to do. I seem to have agreed to be a public channel,
tackling the most unusual of subjects.

After reading all of these essays on celebrity, I am already changing
my ways. I actually turned off an entertainment news show the other
night as they were covering the attempted suicide of Michael Jackson's

daughter. I look at all this with a new vision now, seeing our part in the destruction of the lives of those beings we call famous. Apparently we shoulder some of the blame for that young woman's struggle through the news shows we watch, the magazines we buy, and the delight we find in hearing juicy gossip about the trials and tribulations of the celebrities we love to love — and to hate. Let's stop this spying and feeding off other's lives and lead our own, focused on our own projects and desires. I was the same as many of you before this book came to me and through me; I watched entertainment shows avidly and found some indefinable delight coursing through my veins at the tales of success and woe flashing across the screen. But it's different for me now, and I hope it will become different for you after you've finished this book and read the stories contained within its pages.

Today's transmission felt disinterested and low in energy. John Lennon's disillusionment came through loud and clear. It really felt like he'd rather be somewhere else. Clearly he struggled with his celebrity in life, living his last years almost as a recluse, but he seems to still bear the wounds of it, even after his death. Before John Lennon speaks his piece, Ananda had a few words to say about my nervousness that the last being might be Jesus as well as some comments about the book itself:

We are now only one person away from the final transmission for this book. We have today's being and tomorrow's being, and we understand your fears around this particular person of whom you speak, our dear and wonderful friend Jesus of the Nazarene. There is no need for you to fear, dear one. Whatever comes through will be the correct personage for this particular project, so do not interfere or intervene with your small thoughts. All will be well, and all is perfectly designed to appeal to many different kinds of beings as they read this book.

We have another personage lined up for you to speak to, lined up to speak to the world, for that is what will happen with these recordings: They will be listened to by many, and they will be pulled apart by many. There is no doubt that there will be some who pick out the seeming errors. The details of your world are so much less important to these beings, so of course, they may make small errors that the ego mind will attack as evidence of their untruth. However, you must understand that so many things that are important to you on the Earth plane are not important to these beings. They have much grander principles in their hearts and minds as they are speaking to you. So there will be these attacks from the outside; it is guaranteed.

There is no way that a book or collection such as this can be accepted into the world without great furor, but we are seeing that as a good point. The furor, the dispute, and the disdain will cause a great rising up of attention and energies focused on this particular material, so we do not see it as negative. We do not see it as negative in any way.

The ego is designed for this attacking nature. It is designed to tear apart that which offers salvation, so there will be no surprise and no judgment of it, for it is merely the ego being the ego. It is as if you are looking at a dog pooping on the sidewalk: You cannot judge it compared to the human who does not do that; it is merely being a dog, and there is no point in judging it. You just deal with the consequences. That is what we will consider the attacks of the ego. The attacks are merely something unpleasant you have to deal with, but it is a reality of that being's nature. That is our take on that.

Do not fear. You are going into this project knowing that it will be ridiculed, knowing that it will be reviled, and knowing that there are going to be many people who are very, very curious about it. There will be two sides to the coin, which is the nature of this place in which you live, this relative world. You cannot have the good without the bad; that is just the way of it. The bad will elevate the good. The bad will draw attention to the good. The bad will emphasize the good. That is our take on the whole story.

So on that note, we talk you down from thinking. We send you back into your mind. We tell you to relax, to offer up your body as a vehicle of communication only, as you have done so many times before. It is greatly appreciated in the spirit world that you are doing this. We all applaud you. If you could hear us, you would know we are cheering you on. We accept your wonderful gift of voice in the world, for it is something that is very necessary right now. Know that you are indeed of great import to the elevation of the vibration of the planet and that all of this work will be greatly appreciated. You will look back on it and wonder at your bravery for doing such a thing. So relax your body, relax your mind, and allow us to take over. Allow the next being to speak.

JOHN LENNON'S MESSAGE

I AM HERE. I am here to share my story of my life and my life's work. I am a writer; I am a singer; I am a purveyor of philosophy. I am John Lennon. I am the being you consider one of the most famous singers in the world, and I am helping here because I am a great bringer of attention. I am a great bringer of attention to the philosophical structure of your society. It is something that I did when I was alive, and it is something I am doing now in my nonphysical experience.

So here I am, standing once again in the limelight, which I never did enjoy too much. I was happy to get out of it when I did. It became far too much of a monster for my liking. When you begin your creative ventures as a young man or a young woman, it feels very exciting to be given this adoration. It feels very exciting to be clamored after and sought after for gigs and for musical venues — these kinds of things. But very soon you are unable to walk to the car. Very soon you are unable to do anything, and of course, in our experience as the Beatles, we were very soon inundated with hordes and crowds and oceans of beings who wished to take a little piece of us.

Early on, that was fun. In the beginning, it was exciting, but it was very difficult to live in that circumstance. It was very difficult to live in that way of travel, that way of working. As our lives went along, we became more and more isolated from reality. We became more and more intrigued with the esoteric, and we went on our journeys into the interior world of spirituality and hallucinogenic drugs, searching for something other than what we had. Ironically, we had what everybody thinks would make you happy, but it did not make us happy at all. It merely made us hide behind high walls and it made us fight among ourselves because we were forced to spend time with people who were within the same mode of operation as us. As a group, we spent far too much time together, working together and trying to produce the music and the money we needed to live the private lives that our celebrity forced us to live. So it was an interesting journey. It was an interesting journey — that's all I can say about it. Most of you know how I felt. I ended up isolating myself.

I had been a pretty unhappy person throughout my life. There's no doubt about it. I was introverted. I was seeking something other than what I was doing; I was always dissatisfied with myself. I was very dissatisfied with the world, and I have to be honest: When it came time to go and I was taken the way I was taken, I was perfectly fine with it. The shock of the shot was disturbing, in that sense, but it was instantaneous death for me, and I was flung into a new experience. Because of my investigations into the nonphysical during my life, it was not a problem at all. I expected — I *knew* — what was happening straight away because I had investigated meditation for many years. I'd investigated the trips of the mind, and it was like an amazing acid trip, really. It was exciting. Of course, the feeling of love that pervades you when you cross over is so magnificent that there is no resistance. There is not one iota of resistance in your consciousness whatsoever. And because I was so well aware of nonphysical experiences, of meditation experiences, I had had encounters of my own with consciousnesses other than mine.

I was not troubled at all by my crossing over. As other beings in this exposition have said, this was an agreement I made. I wanted to leave Earth early; I was done with it. I had no desire to stay there. I was disillusioned with it and had done the work I was assigned to do, so it was time for me to leave. I had, in my previous connection in the spiritual world, before I was born, decided that I would be going in this form, in this that is very difficult for people to understand. Of course, from our point of view here, in the nonphysical, death is merely brief event that can carry a message or not. I wanted mine to carry a message because life did not hold for me the illusion of grandeur that it holds for so many of you.

I am happy to be on this side, and I have been told that this is it; I do not need to incarnate again in a physical form, and for that I am very grateful because I am happy here. I am not enamored with the physical or the material, and that is why my life had its challenges — because I wanted out sooner. The last few years were painful for me in the sense that I did not want anything from the world and I felt the world had nothing to give me. So when I came here, it was such a relief, man. What a relief it was to have the freedom to play music, to create music, and to share my vision of love with other beings of like minds! Here, we resonate with love. We love each other, we communicate with each other, we create with each other, and we learn more and more about the universe.

We learn more and more about music, the manifestations of tone, and the octaves of love as they manifest here on the nonphysical side of what you call death.

I am creating and composing all the time here with these beings of like mind. I do work with Earth, but even now I am not enamored of it. I get in discussions here with beings who wish for me to participate in earthly organizations from this nonphysical standpoint, but I am not interested. I am happy to be doing what I am doing here and sharing my little bit of knowledge, my little bit of experience, with other beings. I help counsel some beings who have come over, who have died from celebrity, and they are very excited to meet me. We have great discussions about the music industry and the pitfalls and the downfalls and the ways in which it can be made better. But I'm not going to make it better.

I work with beings who are going to go back and have other incarnations, but I do not wish for that experience. I am more interested in what is going on here in the other levels and other realms of this nonphysical. There are so many things to do, so many things to learn, and so many places to go. There are techniques, practices, and information sources available here that are endless, stimulating, and exciting. There are ways of healing people who have struggled on Earth, so that is really where I shine. I struggled so much on Earth myself with celebrity and disillusionment that this is a much better place for me. This is much more my home; I am more suited to it.

There are beings who come over who want to go back, and we spend some time discussing music, creativity, and what they can do in that realm. We spend some time discussing ways of avoiding the pitfalls of fame while making yourself successful with your own music, with your own designs and creativity that you come up with. That is one of the reasons I am participating in this book.

I want all of you who participate in the celebrity machine, who clamor and claw at the beings who are famous for their creative talents, to treat these beings with love and civility. I ask you not to purchase the "rag mags" that force the paparazzi to take their pictures. This is one of the biggest areas of distress when you are famous, this endless line of photographers outside of your front door who have nothing better to do than feed off the voracious hunger of the crowds of people who buy these magazines. When you purchase that magazine at a check out counter, you cause someone's life to become hellish. When you watch entertainment shows about the strife and struggle celebrities go through, you feed this machine that, in the end, kills us.

That is my message: I would like you to support us through purchasing our music in a civil and respectful way. I would like you to support creative people by purchasing a ticket to their concerts and allowing them to express themselves in a safe and entertaining way. But I ask you, from my heart, as someone who is no longer willing to come back into this world that you've created with this mindset, to back off from the consumption of these products that cause the death of your fellow human beings. There are no two ways about it; that is the consequence of your behavior, and you will be held accountable after your instruction in this subject because you are causing it. It does not matter that it is inadvertent; you know that it is not healthy. You can feel that it is not healthy. It is like peeking under someone's skirt: You know not to do it. If you do it, you are choosing to do it.

That is my take on this whole game. I am happy, on some level, to participate in this book, although even doing this reminds me of what I don't like about planet Earth, what I don't like about the material world. So this will be my last excursion into it, but I really felt that I should join in this creation just to share my story and to let you know that the money you pass across the counter for those "rag mags" — those newspapers and those pictures you love so much — that you feed your ego with, kills people, and there are no two ways about it. It kills people.

So that's my story. It's not a glamorous one, it's not a happy one, but I'm happy now and I'm doing well. I am doing everything I could ever want to do now, with peace and love in my heart, for that was my message in the end. Give peace a chance, and all you need is love — that is the truth of the matter. All you need is love — that is the message of this book. That is the message of this existence. Stay out of your ego, and get going on what you love with the people you love. Make love, not war; make music, not hatred. Be kind to each other, and back off from the celebrities. Just go and see them when they're at a concert. That's okay. Read a book if they write one, but leave them alone. They are just people trying to live their lives, and they don't need you all clamoring at their energy, clamoring at their bodies, scaring them, and, in the end, killing them. That's it. That's all I have to say.

JESUS
CHRIST
c. 6 BCE–c. 30

Jesus founded Christianity, one of the world's most influential religions. His teachings and life are recorded in the Bible's New Testament and emulated by Christians all over the world.

TINA'S COMMENTS

FOR THE PAST FEW DAYS, as Ananda has been giving me a countdown to the end of the book, I have had a nagging thought in the back of my mind: *Please don't let the last person be Jesus. Please don't let the last person be Jesus! I don't want to have to deal with that burden.* After all, that's the final nail in the coffin of insanity in our culture, isn't it? Talking to Jesus. He's the last bastion of the sacred that must not be approached. Trust me, I did not want to approach it or him. I was hoping for Gandhi or Elvis. But really, that's the point of this book — isn't it? — that the nonphysical is real, that it's ours to connect with, and that death is not what we think it is.

Sure enough, this morning my worst fears came true. But as I sit with that experience of putting voice to this one celebrity who has been so very famous, so very worshipped, is it so different, really? After all, the message of this book is that fame is manufactured, that we are all equal in the eyes of Spirit — or God, if you want to use that word. Is this last chapter really so very different, or are the stories around him just older, more well established, and, as history has shown, more dangerous to alter or question? It seems that once the communication is set up between our physical world and that of the nonphysical, it is a no-holds-barred situation — at least as I seem to experience it.

Ananda has warned me to hold on to my hat and prepare for the spotlight to shine on me. Whether that will transpire or not, I don't know. I'll be happy with selling some books and doing some lectures on all this. So far, Ananda have been pretty accurate, so I think I'll take their advice and prepare — just a little. They have said that the message of truth contained in this book will be picked up by default, as people buy this book to find out what Michael, Diana, and Marilyn have to say. Personally, I think it's a brilliant truth-marketing strategy, and I hope it works. Practicing these principles of forgiveness of self and others to the best of my ability has truly changed my world, and I hope that if you are reading this book — even if it's for no other reason than to check out these celebrity communications — you hear the deeper message contained within its pages.

I offer you this information as it came to me, without elaboration, and I cannot prove it or explain it, and I will not try. All I know is that intelligence and personalities that are not my own have visited me each morning for the past four weeks, and because they have been introduced and presented by Ananda, the group of teachers I have come to love and trust with all my heart, I accept them as who and what they say they are. I am personally disappointed that there are not more minorities represented, but perhaps that lack only reflects the imbalance in North America's history and the past lack of power those beings experienced. I don't know. I can only suppose that this particular arrangement of beings is perfect for the purposes designed in the nonphysical.

As I write this, Jesus has begun to teach and speak through me on a daily basis, and he has said that he will do this in public — continue to teach, bringing his word once more, so that we can help ourselves out of the difficulties we find ourselves in. This is not a job I asked for or really wanted; it has just happened, and I have no idea what it will look like or entail.

He dictates his autobiography every morning, which details his life from beginning to end and covers a lot of the incidents in the Bible, but more interestingly, the many years that have no written records at all: his teens and twenties, his relationship with Mary Magdalene, his travels to India, and much more. Today, in fact, as I run through my final edits and comments, he — Jesus — has assigned me some homework. I am to read the New Testament. Apparently this is to give me some foundation in the Bible's teachings so that I can understand more clearly the mindset of people who see this as the truth and who I may encounter as I travel down this road. It's funny — as a teenager I tried to read the Bible once, but I didn't get much past the beginning chapters. It's a tough read, but Jesus assures me it is necessary.

I am told that I have done this work in many lifetimes, according to Ananda and Jesus, but I have no conscious recollection of that. All I know is that I am willing, and apparently able, to translate thought forms from the nonphysical into a format that we all can understand and, perhaps, if we are diligent and willing, put into practice in our lives.

JESUS'S MESSAGE

I AM HERE TO SHARE WITH YOU MY LOVE, my joy, my peace, and my offerings of wisdom. I am indeed this being you would call the Christ — Jesus Christ. I am this being who has walked on this Earth and continues to walk on this Earth, holding your hand through all of your trials and tribulations. There is not one of you who is alone on this journey. I am with you, and when you call my name, I am there at your side, holding your hand. I have many assistants, and they too shall come when you call my name. They too shall come to assist you in your own growth, your own understanding, and your own self-development.

I am here to speak the truth of this world, which is that it is not your natural home. It is not the place where you feel at peace; it is not the place where you feel the love, joy, and magnificence of this universe that has so much to offer you, so much to give you that wishes to flow to you every minute of every day. It is your minds that get in the way of this wonderful communion, and it is your minds that get in the way of this connection to love, this connection to the magnificence of the universe in which you find yourselves.

There are many levels of development in this realm of consciousness. There are lower realms that many of you have never been to. These are the dark and difficult places of minds in deep trauma, deep hatred, and deep fear. Many of you reading this book or listening to this recording have never been to those places, for you were born of the light and did not choose to go down into the darker realms. But there are beings who have done so. There are beings who have made negative choice after negative choice, and they have descended down the steps into what you would consider hell, not knowing that they were doing it themselves, that they create their own destiny, as you all do with your thoughts.

Every single thought you have attracts another thought that is like itself, and this is the message that I wish to bring to you. I have this awareness; I had this awareness on Earth. I was imparted with a wisdom that was divine in nature. It came down into me. I had been an ordinary being, such as yourself, an ordinary man making my own mistakes, making my own errors, living my own ego-centered life in the physical body. I was gifted with an imparting of wisdom that was magnificence, complete awakening, complete knowing.

I saw through my own eyes, my own physical eyes, my senses, the world as it appears to be, and then I saw it as it truly is, which is an energetic mixture of particles and elements that respond to the slightest thought from you, to the slightest feeling from you. These are the truths of the matter, and as you travel through your world, as you travel through your life, you affect every single thing you see. You make every single thing different by your observation of it.

This is why the practices of forgiveness and love are so important in your world. It is why the practice of clarification of the mind is so important, for you have been taught many things that are untrue, and from those untruths rise thoughts and feelings that distort the world in a way that is not to your benefit and causes you much suffering.

All of the suffering you see in the world, all of the suffering that you feel in your mind, is of your own creation, and this is a hard lesson to hear. It is a hard lesson in the beginning, for those of you who have never heard this story, to understand. But you have had many beings now telling you this in the form of this book, under the cover of this book, and I wish for you to understand that this is the message. This is the one message that you must understand: Transform your life and raise yourself up into the realms of love, wisdom, and creativity. Raise yourself up into the realms of that which you would consider angelic and light-infused spiritual realms, which are your home, which are the places you are supposed to create. These are the places where those beings who have understood this principle reside, creating that which they choose, experiencing that which they choose, and assisting beings who are not yet there in their own growth and development.

You must understand that as you observe anything in your world, as you interact with anything in your world, it is the feeling of love that pervades your open mind and heart that will transform it into that which you choose to experience. When you have feelings of love, compassion, and forgiveness, when you understand that this world is your own creation, you will transport yourself into the realms of the magical, into the world of the miracle, and you will transport your body into the world of the immortal. That is the truth of the matter, for all of the physical world that you see, that you have been taught is hard and fast in its manifestation, is no such thing. It is dynamic and liquid in its form, and every time you look at it, every time you touch it, every time you think about it, whatever the subject is, you transform it into something else, given the vibration of your thought and feeling.

It is with this message that I end this book, for you look on the celebrities in your world with a voracious hunger that instills in them a feeling of loss and imbalance, and it hurts them. It hurts their ability to live within their bodies, to learn their lessons, and to find their spiritual paths. I ask you to begin to focus your attention on only that which you love, only that which you care for. And as you do that, as you begin to focus your conscious attention on the creations of your own mind, I ask you to begin to expand your vision of love from those who are your closest family and friends who are easy to love. I ask you to begin to expand your loving thoughts and presence out into those realms that you do not currently love.

I ask you to begin to see the soldiers of war in the enemy countries against whom your country is fighting as souls who are doing what they have been taught. They are doing what their teachers, parents, and political leaders have taught them is the right thing to do. Forgive them. I ask you to pray for them, to send love to them, for this is the act that will change the state of war on your planet.

I ask you to buy only healthy foods that will nurture these bodies in which you find yourselves, for they are the vehicles of transformation, the vehicles that provide you with the experiences that allow you to develop your spiritual awareness, your spiritual nature. Eventually you will not need these bodies, but for now you do, so I ask you to pay attention to what you put into them. Do not poison them with drugs and alcohol that do not serve the higher purposes you have designed for your lives. Do not fill them with foods that are corrupted by the financial and food manufacturing systems of your planet. Feed them with healthy food that loves your cellular structure. Feed your bodies with healthy water that nourishes each atom and element. Feed them with wonderful, fresh, and vibrant vegetables and fruits that are free of contamination, and offer up this wonderful nutrition for your spiritual growth and your spiritual edification.

Look around you at those beings who are suffering, and if you cannot offer them material assistance, then offer them your love, your light, your thought, and your heart, for that is what will truly lift them up out of the depths of the sadness in which they find themselves. If you have a friend who is depressed, take some time out of your day to offer them prayers and thoughts of love and light, and ask my assistance in their healing, for I will come at my name's call. You must understand this: that the nonphysical is pervasive in its nature. We hear every single thought you have. We hear every single prayer you utter, and do not think that we do not listen. You must understand this principle — that every thought you have, every feeling you have, every emotion you have, every word you speak, and every action you take creates the world you see on the outside of your current body that you feel is you.

This body is not you. The entire world is you. The entire planet is you expressing yourself. Each one of you expresses yourself, and that is manifesting in the world, so you can see there is much work to be done. Each one of you has the ability to transform the world through the transformation of your own mind. You have the ability to connect with endless sources of inspiration and energy. You have the ability to connect with endless good health, love, abundance, and sweet connection with other beings through your thought processes. It is through the ideas and beliefs that run through your mind that you will make this connection.

There is much action you can take in the world, but if that action is based on incorrect and unloving thoughts, it will not achieve the higher goals you have set for yourself in your pre-life contract. You wish to achieve enlightenment. You wish to achieve the waking up of your entire self, which is a magnificent being. You look at me and the stories you hear of me, and you think that this is an impossibility — that I am a divine creation, separate from you, different in all ways — and that is not the truth.

I was an ordinary man. I was a man, a woman — such as you living in a physical body, living an ordinary life, and I was gifted with the awakening and knowledge, the awareness of how things work on your plane, and I ran with that knowledge. I took it unto my heart and worked with it in my incarnation on this plane, and as I developed this skill, as I developed this connection, I continued my work after my passing. I continued to develop this and to work with the higher realms, and I have become what you would consider a lightbeing, a being of extreme translucence, a being of extreme energy, a being of extreme understanding and wisdom. And I have dedicated my life to assisting all of you in this journey.

The stories that are told about my divinity being above yours are not true. I am no more divine than you. You each have the ability to achieve that which I achieved. I was blessed with immersion in the truth as a gift from the higher realms. It was done in one motion, but I still had to work with my humanity. I still had to work within the constraints of my physical body to pass the message along. It was distorted and changed over the centuries, but this is the message I wish to give to you, the message I wish for you to understand: You are the Creator, physically manifested in this pointed form of experience, this focused form of interpretation that is the human mind, and you are endowed with all of the magnificence of the Creator's ability to manufacture experiences, relationships, and these objective things in the world, these things you call objects. They are manufactured within the mind you possess, and it is this that is so important for you to understand.

I do not wish for my name to taint this text. The channel was quite worried I would show up and speak my piece and add an element of "unreality" to this book, but the truth of the matter is we are all the same. We are all on the journey to elevation; we are all on the journey to heaven; we are all on the journey to self-realization and understanding this universe, and I am no different. I place myself among ordinary human beings as a testament to this reality — that I am no different from you. I am merely somebody who understood the technical operations and the way the universe works, the way creation works, and the way healing works: through the mind and heart working in concert, in alignment with truth. And the truth of that is all is love.

All of the things you see around you in your world that are not of love are *not* created by that which you call God. They are created by the lower realms of the human mind, which you call the ego, and that is what causes your suffering. You are a blending of the light and the dark. You are a blending of the ego and spirit, and it is only through focusing your mind on that which is spirit, on that which is of the higher vibration, that you will transform your life into that which is a miracle, into that which is in the realm of the elevated, angelic, miraculous, and powerful.

You all want this. You all want to experience this, and you are all capable, but you must break your unhealthy habits of thought. You must break your unhealthy habits of drinking and eating and drugging, and you must focus your attention on that which is love. You must focus your attention on that which is kindness. You must focus your attention on that which is forgiveness for all the sins you perceive as having been committed against you, for they have not been committed against you; they were creations of your own mind manifesting in the world to show you where you are off track, where your internal thoughts are incorrect. The hatreds that have been perpetrated on you are the expression of hatreds that are contained within your mind, and that is the truth of the matter. That is the truth I wish to bring to you: that everything you see, that everything you experience in your world is a belief of your own created in the physical for you to understand and to transform.

Look at your life. Look at that expression that is your life — your body, your work, your friends and family, your country of origin — and look around. If you see something you do not like, figure out what it is. Is it hatred? Is it judgment? Is it narrow-mindedness? Is it weakness? Whatever it is that is manifesting in your world, go inside and seek out that aspect of yourself that is contained within your beliefs and your thoughts, and begin to investigate it. Begin to heal it, for it is there that the healing will take place, and it is in that internal healing and this understanding I am sharing with you that you will transform the world in which you live, just as I transformed the world in which I lived.

I understood the process, and I employed it in my daily life. That is what *you* must do. This is what the path to salvation is: It is understanding the creative process, understanding that you are the Creator manifested in a physical body, expressing Itself, coming to understand Itself, and healing Itself. As you raise your vibration up and as you transform, initially, your own internal world, that will then begin to manifest in your external world, and you will eventually begin to transform the world. If you all do this in concert, if you all do this together, if you all do this as a statement of your desire for a transformed world, then indeed the world will transform. It will have no choice, for you are the ones who create it. You are the ones who create the good, the bad, and the ugly in this world in which you exist.

There are many other realms you will move on to once you have finished in this one, but you cannot move on until you have cleansed your heart, soul, and mind of the untruths that exist within your heart, within your belief systems, and within your thought processes. You must cleanse yourself — not as a moral judgment but as an understanding of the way this universe creates. It creates through thought, focus, and emotion, and it is within your power to create the world that you wish for.

That is all I have to say for now. I hope my name being added to this list of the famous and the infamous will not detract from the message. I hope it will add to the message. I hope it will create a groundswell of interest in this book that will begin to transform the world. You all need to focus on your own creations; you all need to focus on loving the world you are in from your own point of view, and you need to change that which you are doing, for your world suffers terribly, and you suffer terribly, and it is unnecessary. It is through your own mistaken judgments, through your own mistaken unforgiveness, and through your own mistaken weakness that you suffer, and it is not necessary. It can change.

Listen to the words in this book. Listen to the words I have spoken, and begin the work of your own healing and transformation. You will begin the work of the healing and transformation of this planet on which you find yourself, for she is in deep need of your assistance. She is in deep need of your transformation, for the practices you indulge in now are killing her, and she will not stand idly by and let it happen. If you do not change your ways, your ways will be changed for you by the natural environment in which you find yourself. Do it voluntarily, do it with love, do it with awareness, and do it with the understanding that this is the desire of the universe — that you act in a loving way to all beings, including yourself, including those you hate, and including the enemies of your country. If you transform your mind, once again you will transform the world, and that is our desire for you. That is our wish for you.

CONCLUSION

ANANDA

YOU HAVE READ THIS BOOK NOW, and you have encountered many famous faces, many famous minds you were somewhat familiar with. Now you have the complete story, the complete interpretation of their experiences of their lives on Earth.

When you observed them, from your point of view, you only had half the story. You only had your interpretation of what their lives meant, what their values were, and what their purposes were. Now you have their true versions of what it meant for them to live the famous lives they experienced, what it felt like to pass over, and what their experiences are like now. You have much information that will assist in you in understanding your own life. You will come to see that there are trials and tribulations in your lives that push you toward transformation, that ask you to shift your consciousness, and we hope this book will assist you in that journey of comprehension, of understanding, of truly seeing what your life is for, what its value is, and what your purpose is here on this planet.

Your purpose is creativity; your purpose is love; your purpose is joy; your purpose is cooperation; your purpose is self-expression. Your purpose is not to follow other beings' lives, voraciously seeking information about them. Your purpose is to create your own life, putting all of your effort, all of your joy, all of your skill, and all of your enthusiasm into manifesting that which you desire, into experiencing that which you desire.

You are often taught in your world to put aside your desires, to not follow your heart — to follow the practical, to follow the prescribed, to follow the organized. We counsel you here to do the opposite. We say to do that which you choose to do, which brings you joy. Do that which fills your heart with wondrous feelings of expansion and self-expression. Do not cow-tow to the powers that be; they do not have your best interests at heart. They have their own pocketbooks and their own power in the backs of their minds as they tell you how to behave.

Begin to misbehave. Begin to follow your own heart's desire. Begin to create the world you wish to experience. Begin to live your true desire from a place of love, self-love, and self-expression. You have the gift of life; you have the gift of this physical body. You have the gift of understanding more and more each day as new information comes to you.

You have not picked up this book by accident; you have not picked up this book for no reason. It has come into your world, into your mind, for a purpose, and that is to shift your beliefs about your life, your death experience, and what the afterlife experience contains, for many of you are constantly afraid of death. You are so afraid of death that you will not live your lives, and what we wish for you to understand is that life is everlasting. It continues on and on. There is no point in procrastinating; there is no point in putting off what you wish to do, for if you do not do it in this life, you will be brought back again to do it in another life.

Take off the limitations of your mind, and begin to see where you are restricted. Begin to see where what you have been taught is not serving you. Begin to make different decisions. Begin to shift your life in a way that is more pleasing. Begin to shift your life in a way that is more self-expressive of who you truly are, and allow that being inside of you — that true self, that loving self, that creative self, that freedom-seeking self — out into the world. Allow that self to stretch his or her limbs, to wake up, look around, and see what is truly there for you.

There is much in this world for you. There are friends; there are lovers; there are wonderful creative outlets that you can follow. Step out of the prisons you have stepped into voluntarily, for nothing keeps you there except your own belief in the bars. Break free of your constraints, break free of your fears, and step into a world that is yours for the taking,

̀urs for the creating, yours for the loving, and yours for the caring for.
ᵣill find that all will go well.

ad this book again if you have just read it once. Read it again.
much wisdom in these pages. Do not skim across it as you do
oks, throwing it on the pile of material read, to be dismissed as
ᵣntertainment. Contained within these pages are the wisdoms of
ᵣny lifetimes, and they offer up their wisdom to you to assist you in
your life, in your decisions, so that you do not have to make the mistakes
they made, getting lost in the mire of the darkness, fear, and destruction
of your modern society.

Step out of the prescribed programming you have participated in
and become free beings, expressing your true nature, expressing your
kind, loving, and creative selves so that the world is enhanced, so that the
world is improved, and so that your life becomes a greater joy than it was
ever imagined in your mind.

We are Ananda. We are your dear friends. We are teachers here to
assist you in your waking up, to assist you in your understanding of what
this world means and how it functions. We hope this text, this book, has
provided you with some tantalizing information and some new ideas
that you may apply to your own existence.

We leave you with love. We leave you with gratitude for sharing your
time with us, and we will speak to you again — another time.

SOURCES

ALL CHAPTERS BEGIN WITH ITALICIZED BIOGRAPHICAL
INFORMATION TAKEN FROM BIOGRAPHY.COM.

Albert Einstein
http://www.biography.com/people/albert-ein-stein-9285408

Gerry Garcia
http://www.biography.com/people/jerry-garcia-9306297

Ralph Waldo Emerson
http://www.biography.com/people/ralph-waldo-emer-son-9287153

Marilyn Monroe
http://www.biography.com/people/marilyn-mon-roe-9412123

John Huston
http://www.biography.com/people/john-huston-9348018

Amy Winehouse
http://www.biography.com/people/amy-wine-house-244469

Margaret Thatcher
http://www.biography.com/people/margaret-thatch-er-9504796

Princess Diana
http://www.biography.com/people/princess-di-ana-9273782

Susan B. Anthony
http://www.biography.com/people/susan-b-antho-ny-194905

Sylvia Plath
http://www.biography.com/people/sylvia-plath-9442550

Elizabeth Taylor
http://www.biography.com/people/elizabeth-tay-lor-37991

Robert Kennedy
http://www.biography.com/people/robert-kenne-dy-9363052

John F. Kennedy
http://www.biography.com/people/john-f-kenne-dy-9362930

Michael Jackson
http://www.biography.com/people/michael-jack-son-38211

Cecil B. DeMille
http://www.biography.com/people/cecil-b-demi-lle-9271261

Jonas Salk
http://www.biography.com/people/jonas-salk-9470147

Queen Mother Elizabeth
http://www.biography.com/people/queen-mother-elizabeth-9286203

George Bernard Shaw
http://www.biography.com/people/george-bernard-shaw-9480925

John Lennon
http://www.biography.com/people/john-lennon-9379045

Jesus Christ
http://www.biography.com/people/jesus-christ-9354382

ABOUT THE AUTHOR

TINA LOUISE SPALDING was born in England in 1958 and immigrated to Canada with her family in 1976. Raised in a family that visited psychics often, she is no stranger to the nonphysical world. But she found the modern world challenging, and at the age of forty-two, after two divorces and with a deep dissatisfaction with modern life, she moved to an island off Canada's west coast to pursue her art and heal.

This was a difficult time for Tina, as she was separated from her two sons, Alex and Kieran. She found solace in the spiritual text *A Course In Miracles* and focused intently on its teachings and practices. After ten years of internal transformations initiated by this book, Tina felt drawn to teach the life-enhancing philosophy in its pages, but she was not prepared for the form that would take.

On the summer solstice of 2012, Tina settled down for an afternoon nap, and began a journey that has culminated in this book. That afternoon, powerful energies began to surge through Tina's body, leading to ecstasy, bliss, and an altered state of consciousness that lasted for almost a month. The feelings finally drove her to take an automatic writing workshop, where she was first made aware of Ananda. She began to write for this group of nonphysical teachers who have come to assist us in our waking process.

Since that time, Tina has begun to speak for Ananda as a full trance channel, offering teachings and personal readings for those who are seeking more happiness, fulfillment, and connection with Spirit. She has dedicated her life to writing and speaking for Ananda and other nonphysical beings, sharing their wisdom and spiritual knowledge.

☀ *Light Technology* PUBLISHING

TOM T. MOORE

THE GENTLE WAY
A SELF-HELP GUIDE FOR THOSE WHO BELIEVE IN ANGELS

This book is for all faiths and beliefs with the only requirement being a basic belief in angels. It will put you back in touch with your guardian angel or strengthen and expand the connection that you may already have. How can I promise these benefits? Because I have been using these concepts for over ten years and I can report these successes from direct knowledge and experience. But this is a self-help guide, so that means it requires your active participation.

$14.⁹⁵ • 140 PP. SOFTCOVER • ISBN 978-1-891824-60-9

THE GENTLE WAY II
BENEVOLENT OUTCOMES: THE STORY CONTINUES

You'll be amazed at how easy it is to be in touch with guardian angels and how much assistance you can receive simply by asking. This inspirational self-help book, written for all faiths and beliefs, will explain how there is a more benevolent world that we can access and how we can achieve this. These very unique and incredibly simple techniques assist you in manifesting your goals easily and effortlessly for the first time. It works quickly, sometimes with immediate results — no affirmations, written intentions, or changes in behavior are needed. You don't even have to believe in it for it to work!

$16.⁹⁵ • 320 PP. SOFTCOVER • ISBN 978-1-891824-80-7

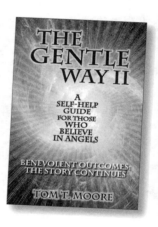

THE GENTLE WAY III
MASTER YOUR LIFE

Almost three years have passed since *The Gentle Way II* was published. Yet as many success stories as that book contained, I have continued to receive truly unique stories from people all over the world requesting most benevolent outcomes and asking for benevolent prayers for their families, friends, other people, and other beings. It just proves that there are no limits to this modality, which is becoming a gentle movement as people discover how much better their lives are with these simple yet powerful requests.

$16.⁹⁵ • 304 PP. SOFTCOVER • ISBN 978-1-62233-005-8

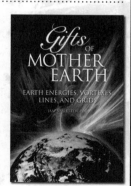